Dear Student,

I see many students who are frustrated and discouraged with their attempts to decide a major or career. I believe part of the problem may be our rather naïve perception that we can do anything if it pays enough money and has enough status.

We probably are capable of doing almost anything we set our minds to. However, knowledge of our personality preferences or True Colors™ will help us understand why we are not motivated to do just anything.

By nature we are motivated toward certain pursuits and not others. Being aware of our personality preferences brings focus and helps us choose careers that will enhance our natural, inherent gifts and talents. Without this knowledge, we remain scattered and unfocused.

This workbook will guide you through this new concept in career decision-making and help you focus on your natural strengths. You will be taken on a journey of self-discovery—one that will lead you in making decisions about meaningful work that allows you to express who you truly are.

I know you will find this experience rewarding if you commit to completing this workbook. You may also want to read the companion book **Follow Your True Colors® To The Work You Love**. In any event, I wish you fun and success as you discover your True Colors and move toward the work you'll love!

Sincerely,

Carolyn Kalil

Carolyn Kalil
Counselor

True Colors

True Colors, Inc. Publishing is pleased to release **Follow Your True Colors To The Work You Love: The Workbook**, by Carolyn Kalil and Don Lowry. **The Workbook** is, in fact, the second edition of Kalil's and Lowry's, **How To Express Your Natural Skills And Talents In A Career**, published by True Colors, Inc. back in 1989. This latest work by the pair has a great new look, and has been fully revised to include updated career information, as well as new proven approaches for career selection developed by Ms. Kalil in the classroom over the last ten years.

As Ms. Kalil wrote in her introductory "Dear Student" letter, **The Workbook** is a companion to her 1998 book, **Follow Your True Colors To The Work You Love**, also published by True Colors, Inc. Publishing. Although each book stands on its own, together they offer a complete and fun course of study for discovering your life's work.

Now, get ready to enjoy discovering your natural strengths and skills, and uncovering your pathway to the work you love.

ISBN 1-893320-20-0

Copy editor: Mike Berry
Book design: Michael Church
Printed and bound by Publishers Press
Second Printing February 2001

TCP218-2

True Colors

Follow Your True Colors To The Work You Love

The Workbook

A journey in self-discovery & career decision-making

Carolyn Kalil & Don Lowry

True Colors, Inc. Publishing
Riverside, California

True Colors

About the Authors

This workbook is the result of the collaborated efforts of Carolyn Kalil and Don Lowry.

Kalil is a counselor at El Camino Community College in Southern California and author of the book **Follow Your True Colors To The Work You Love**.

Lowry is the president of True Colors, Inc. in Laguna Beach, California and the developer of True Colors®.

www.truecolorscareer.com
carolyn@truecolorscareer.com

Table of Contents

True Colors

Preface

Why I wrote this workbook

A majority of students I have counseled since 1973 have expressed a fear of investing time, energy, and money toward making the wrong career choice. Time and again, they demonstrated strong resistance to spending several years in college preparing for a career they did not feel highly motivated to pursue. And their counseling sessions typically ended up focusing on a career decision, regardless of the initial reason for the appointment.

On many occasions, these students have come to me with personal problems related to study habits, but the nature of their problem was generally the same: They had lost interest in school because of indecision as to their futures. These students lacked direction and found it difficult to focus on school and studies. Some were experiencing conflicts with parents, family, and spouses as a result of dropping grades and lack of motivation.

A knowledge of personality preferences through the True Colors™ model has helped me tremendously in understanding the natural gifts, talents, and values of students and directing them toward careers they will find truly satisfying. Its clear, definitive methods for finding success and enhancing self-esteem are invaluable. And once you begin this workbook, I am confident you will want to integrate the True Colors™ program into your academic, personal, and career endeavors. It will be a journey well worth your time and effort and will impact all segments of your life.

Additional workbooks, booklets, manuals, and catalogs can be obtained by calling True Colors, Inc. at (800) 422-4686.

True Colors

There is only one success — to be able to spend your life in your own way.

— Christopher Morley

Chapter
1

INTRODUCTION

Chapter 1

Introduction

Theoretical Base

This workbook is based on the belief that we have intrinsic characteristics which drive our human behavior and through which we strive to experience self-esteem. As a result, we are imprinted with specific ways of thinking, understanding, valuing, and conceptualizing.

Our behavior, therefore, manifests certain attitudes, preferences, wants, aims, needs, motives, and desires that make us feel good about ourselves. These predispositions drive our actions and habits, making our behavior predictable in all contexts of our lives.

This theory of individual differences is not new and traces to Hippocrates, who 25 centuries ago identified four different types of human beings in his 1921 release of **Psychological Type**.

Soon after, Isabel Myers Briggs developed the now famous **Myers Briggs Type Indicator** which states that human behavior is quite orderly and can be characterized by 16 different personality types.

Dr. David Keirsey has been refining the work of Myers Briggs for the past 35 years. His book, **Please Understand Me**, reflects the basis of the "True Colors" philosophy.

Don Lowry, my co-author, uses True Colors as a metaphor for understanding human characteristics and how intrinsic behavior must be differentially rewarded. He uses green, blue, orange, and gold—colors that will be used herein to represent each temperament type.

True Colors in comparison to Keirsey's temperament language:		
Blue	=	**NF**
Green	=	**NT**
Gold	=	**SJ**
Orange	=	**SP**

The Meaning Behind the Colors of "True Colors"

Color has long been used as a component of our association and learning process. The physiological impulses generated by certain colors have a marked influence on our lives and can unconsciously mold and guide us in varied directions.

Manufacturers of goods and services recognize the effects of color in regard to marketing products and industrial designers set the moods of working environments with the use of color. Color can relieve tension and stress and assist in creating tranquil surroundings. It is fitting that the color association concept be adopted in the learning process in lieu of highly technical formulas, symbols, and alphabetical and numerical designations.

Throughout this workbook, you will be constantly fortified with the significance of the four basic colors and their relationship to the subject matter discussed.

Green: Green expresses itself psychologically as the will in operation; as perseverance and tenacity. Green is an expression of firmness and constancy. It indicates constancy of viewpoint as well as constant self-awareness. Green places a high value on the "I" in all forms of possession and self-affirmation.

Persons with green as a primary color want to increase certainty of their own values. They accomplish this either through assertiveness (by holding fast to an idealized perception they have of themselves), or through acknowledgment from others in deference to their possessions—whether greater wealth, or superiority in physical, educational, or cultural attainment.

Blue: Blue represents complete calm. Contemplation of this color effectively pacifies the central nervous system. Blue, like all four basic colors, is a chromatic representation of a basic biological need—in this case, a physiological tranquillity and a psychological contentment equating to peace and gratification.

Those with blue as a primary color live with balance and harmony and are free of tension; they feel settled, united, and secure.

Blue represents the bands one draws around oneself and others–a sense of connection. But when allies are involved, blues are especially vulnerable. Consequently, blue corresponds to depth of feeling. Blue, as a relaxed sensitivity, is a prerequisite for empathy, for aesthetic experience, and for meditative awareness.

Orange: Orange represents an energy-expending physiological condition. It is the expression of vital force and of nervous and glandular activity. Thus, it holds the meaning of desire and of all forms of appetite and craving.

Orange is the urge to achieve results and win success; it is hungry to desire all of those things that offer intensity of living and fullness of experience.

Orange is impulse, the will to win, and all forms of vitality and power from sexual potency to revolutionary transformation. It is the impulse toward active doing, toward sport, struggle, competition, eroticism, and enterprising productivity. As impact of the will or the force of will, it corresponds symbolically to the blood of conquest, to the sanguine temperament, and to masculinity. Its sensory perception is appetite; its emotional content is desire; and its organs are the voluntary muscles, the sympathetic nervous system, and the organs of reproduction.

In temporal terms, Orange is the present.

Gold: Gold is sensation as it applies to the bodily senses. It represents a need to be responsible, to fulfill duties and obligations, to organize and to structure lives.

Gold is practical sensibility and punctuality; it is the belief that people should earn their way in life through work and service to others. Gold reflects a need to belong and an effort to carry a share of the load in all areas of living. It is stability, maintained organization, efficiency, and strong concept of home and family—faithful, loyal, and dependable.

How does this color theory impact career planning? If differences make behavior predictable in all contexts, this would also hold true in career decision-making. The subsequent chapters will assist each of the color groups in making career decisions that are consistent with who they are.

True Colors

A Career Versus A Job

A career is much more than a job. A job is a series of tasks performed for pay, usually without much preparation or concern for personal growth or enjoyment.

A career, on the other hand, encompasses all of the job characteristics, and more. One needs to prepare for a career by obtaining required training or education. A career accounts for who a person is, making personality, interests, values, and skills integral parts of a career decision. These considerations allow a career-minded person to continue to grow and to develop, thereby encouraging individual expression and enhanced satisfaction in one's work.

Why Plan A Career?

Generally speaking, most working Americans do not enjoy the work they do. This is because they have chosen a job rather than plan a career that expresses who they are. Since most of us will work 40 hours each week the majority of our lives, the quality of our lives depends greatly on what we do during those precious hours.

The most important component of career planning involves self-understanding. The following chapters will help you understand yourself more thoroughly than ever before. Then you will gather occupational information to assist you in making decisions and setting goals toward a career that can become your life's work.

True Colors

Ours is a world where people don't know what they want and are willing to go through hell to get it.

— Don Marquis

Exercise 1

Pre-test

How well do you know your strengths? You began this workbook with certain beliefs about the things that you do well. List below all the things you are good at doing. You will learn more later in this workbook about your real strengths.

My strengths are:

1.

2.

3.

4.

5.

6.

7.

8.

9.

10.

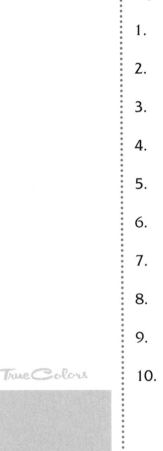

Exercise 2

Criteria for selecting a career

Extrinsic factors
(those that satisfy
external needs)

Intrinsic factors
(those that satisfy
deeper personal needs)

1.   1.

2.   2.

3.   3.

4.   4.

5.   5.

"For a career to be satisfying and have a sense of purpose, extrinsic factors need to be secondary to intrinsic factors."

1-minute essay
Discuss why you agree or disagree with the above statement

_____

_____

_____

_____

_____

_____

True Colors

Exercise 3

Outstanding attributes

List your outstanding attributes.

My name:

My outstanding attributes:_____

_____

_____

_____

_____

_____

_____

Write the name of someone you know and list their outstanding attributes.

Name:

Attributes:_____

_____

_____

_____

_____

_____

True Colors

Write a one-minute essay explaining which list is longer. Why?

_____

_____

_____

_____

_____

Exercise 4

What does success mean to you?

_____

_____

_____

_____

_____

_____

Success is a public affair, failure is a private funeral.

— Rasalind Russel

True Colors

Nothing succeeds like success.

— Alexander Dumas

_____

_____

_____

_____

_____

Exercise 5

Spending your money

Congratulations! You have just won the 10 million-dollar lottery. Now what will you do with your time? Describe the kind of work you would do to make a contribution to society.

_____

_____

_____

_____

_____

_____

_____

_____

_____

True Colors

Which of these things could you begin doing now?

_____

_____

_____

_____

_____

_____

_____

Exercise 6

Where are you now?

What are some of the college majors you have considered?

_____

_____

_____

How do you presently feel about each one?

_____

_____

_____

What subjects do you enjoy most?

_____

_____

_____

Why did you make the decision to go to college?

_____

_____

_____

_____

_____

How committed are you to staying in school?

_____

_____

_____

_____

Who is supporting you in reaching your goals?

_____

_____

_____

True Colors

Chapter 1

Short Journal (5 minutes or less)

Do you feel your life is moving in the direction you want it to go? Why or Why not?

_____

_____

_____

_____

_____

_____

_____

_____

_____

_____

_____

_____

_____

_____

_____

True Colors

Knowing others is wisdom. Knowing the self is enlightenment.

— Lao-tzu

Chapter 2

WHO AM I?

Chapter 2

Who am I?

I cannot stress enough the value in understanding yourself as the first step in career decision-making. This knowledge allows you to direct your energies, focus your attention, and find a career that is compatible and satisfying.

This chapter, as well as the following three, will focus on self-understanding. Without such an understanding, career planning would be like reading want ads without knowing which offering best suits you. Instead, you must determine those things you are naturally inspired to do—what you spend time doing because you enjoy it, not because you are being paid to perform or produce.

I believe we all have natural gifts and talents which can lead us in the direction of an enjoyable and fulfilling career. But all too often, someone close to us convinces us we cannot do something, or we are unable to overcome fears about pursuing a certain goal. Whatever the reason, we must ask ourselves how much it is worth to go for what we really want.

For an understanding of what it is like to be engaged in dissatisfying work, simply observe employees at some of the local businesses you frequent. Do they exhibit a lack of enthusiasm? Is their service courteous? You can avoid such pitfalls by learning to make career decisions based on who you are, what you enjoy doing, and your natural strengths.

However, some people base their career decisions solely on income. While income is a natural consideration when planning a career, I believe that those persons creative enough to base a career on what they enjoy doing will also use that creativity to ensure sufficient financial reward. An example is the young man who told me he enjoyed wrecking his toys as a young boy and now is very successful in the demolition business.

On the next page, you can begin your journey of self-understanding—a journey that will lead you in the direction of an exciting career.

True Colors

It is not easy to find happiness in ourselves, and it is not possible to find it elsewhere.

— Agnes Repplier

Because families have a major impact on shaping our lives, writing about our past can help us understand who we are as a result of those experiences. Complete the following exercises and begin to better understand yourself!

Exercise 1

Family experiences

Describe your home experience as a child. Include such things as how many children in your family, birth order, your general emotional state (happy, sad, etc.), your relationship with each parent.

_____

_____

_____

_____

_____

_____

_____

_____

_____

_____

True Colors

Give a little love to a child, and you get a great deal back.

— John Ruskin

What messages did you receive about who you are from your parents and other family members?

Parents must get across the idea that "I love you always, but sometimes I do not love your behavior."

— Amy Vanderbilt

_____

_____

_____

_____

_____

_____

_____

_____

Exercise 2

Beliefs

What is the relationship between what you learned about yourself from your family members and your own beliefs about yourself today?

_____

_____

_____

_____

_____

_____

_____

True Colors

***Man is what
he believes***

— Anton Chekhov

Which beliefs do not serve you and need to be changed? (In a later chapter you will learn how to change negative thought patterns into positive ones.)

Beliefs

1.

2.

3.

4.

5.

6.

7.

8.

9.

10.

Chapter 2

Short Journal (5 minutes or less)

Write about something you have learned about yourself.

_____

_____

_____

_____

True Colors

*The cards you hold
in the game of life means
very little—it's the way
you play that counts.*

Chapter

3

MY TRUE COLORS

Chapter 3

My True Colors

The following exercise will introduce you to True Colors and assist you on a journey of knowing who you are. This knowledge will allow you to be an active participant in life rather than a passenger or a bystander.

Exercise 1

Identifying Your True Colors

Step 1: Visualize Yourself

As you read the following passages, look closely at the corresponding color illustrations on the front of each Character Card. (Cards included.) Do not yet turn over the cards.

Green: "I have this new program for making the organization run like clockwork. Thirty-five years of research, coupled with a computerized network of state-of-the-art equipment will give us a head start on the new program . . ." (New ideas, new technology.)

Blue: "I realize that good material is very necessary to start, but we have to consider the personnel. They have their rights too, you know. After all, Harry's feelings should be considered before starting this program—or anything, for that matter . . ." (Feeling, compassionate, adaptable.)

Orange: "As I see it, the world belongs to those who take action, and 'action' is my middle name! By the time the organizers have it organized, I'll have it done and be ready for something new. So, whattaya say? Let's start now . . ." (Impulsive, immediate, independent.)

Gold: "I think a clear-cut, down-to-business mode will get us to the bottom line here. After all, this institution has been here longer than the rest of us and it is our responsibility to see that promises are kept and that the program runs smoothly . . ." (Responsible, practical, need to belong.)

Now that you are familiar with at least a few of the color group characteristics, rank the cards from the one that is most like you to the one that is least like you.

True Colors

Carmen   May 8, 2002

Step 2: Read About Yourself

Turn over the Character Cards and read the back of each. Arrange them again from the one most like you to the one least like you. Rank them in the boxes below using a "4" for the card most like you down to a "1" for the card least like you.

COURAGEOUS	CONVENTIONAL	COMPASSIONATE	CONCEPTUAL
1	2	3	4

Step 3: Describe Yourself

Below are several rows of word groups. Working one row at a time, rank each word group in the boxes using a "4" for the group most like you down to a "1" for the word group least like you. (Score words across.)

Active Opportunistic Spontaneous		Parental Traditional Responsible		Authentic Harmonious Compassionate		Versatile Inventive Competent	
	2		3		4		1
Competitive Impetuous Impactful	3	Practical Sensible Dependable	1	Unique Empathetic Communicative	4	Curious Conceptual Knowledgeable	2
Realistic Open-minded Adventuresome	4	Loyal Conservative Organized	1	Devoted Warm Poetic	2	Theoretical Seeking Ingenious	3
Daring Impulsive Fun	1	Concerned Procedural Cooperative	3	Tender Inspirational Dramatic	2	Determined Complex Composed	4
Exciting Courageous Skillful	3	Orderly Conventional Caring	1	Vivacious Affectionate Sympathetic	2	Philosophical Principled Rational	4
Total Orange	14	Total Gold	11	Total Blue	17	Total Green	18

True Colors

Scoring Your True Colors

Now that you have sorted your Character Cards and discovered and read about yourself, have you identified your color spectrum?

Write your color spectrum below. If you are unable to do so at this point, try repeating the process for additional clarity. Or, you may wish to ask people who know you well just how they see you.

My brightest color:

_____
(The color of your highest total)

My brightest color is shaded with:

_____
(The color of your second highest total)

And

_____
(The color of your second lowest total)

With

_____
(A pale color of your lowest total)

You now know your brightest color, the one which most esteems you. The values of your shaded colors vary in importance and the values of your most pale color are least expressed in your behavior.

Using Your Cards With Others

Keep your Character Cards to use with others. Your friends will have a natural interest in playing True Colors with you. And once you understand their True Colors spectrum, you can utilize the keys to improve communication, as well as your personal, academic, and professional success.

Now, continue reading about your spectrum on the following pages.

The Color Spectrum

Green

Your strength is knowledge! You feel best about yourself when solving problems and when your ideas are recognized, especially when you feel ingenious. You seek to express yourself through your ability to be an expert in everything.

You are a complex individualist with great analytical ability. Your idea of a great day is to use your know-how to create solutions. Although you do not express your emotions openly, you do experience deep feelings.

Your Keys To Personal Success:

Developing models	Abstract thinking
Analytical processes	Exploring ideas
A variety of interests	Striving for competency
Admiring intelligence	Storing wisdom and knowledge
Being a perfectionist	Abhorring redundancy
Utilizing precise language	Handling complexity

You Tend To:

Dream of:	Truth, perfection, accuracy
Value:	Answers, resolutions, intelligence, explanations
Regard:	Efficiency, increased output, reduced waste
Dislike:	Injustice and unfairness
Express:	Coolness, calm, and collected reservation
Foster:	Inventions and technology
Respect:	Knowledge and capability
Promote:	Effectiveness, competence, and know-how

True Colors

Knowledge is power.

Blue

Your strength is authenticity! If your brightest color is blue, you seek to express the inner you. Authenticity and honesty are valued above all other characteristics. You are sensitive to subtlety and - with great flair - you create roles in life's drama. You enjoy close relationships with those you love, and you possess a strong spirituality in your nature.

Making a difference in the world is easy for you because you cultivate the potential in yourself and in others.

Your Keys To Personal Success:

Authenticity as a standard	Seeking reality
Devotion to relationships	Cultivating potential of others
Assuming creative roles in life's drama	Writing and speaking with poetic flair
Self-searching	Having a life of significance
Sensitivity to subtlety	Spirituality
Making a difference in the world	Seeking harmony

You Tend To:

Dream of:	Love, affection, and authenticity
Value:	Compassion, sympathy, and rapport
Regard:	Meaning, significance, and identity
Dislike:	Hypocrisy, deception, and insincerity
Express:	Vivacity, enthusiasm, and inspiration
Foster:	Potential growth in people and harmony
Respect:	Nurturing, empathy, and sharing of feelings
Promote:	Growth and development in others

True Colors

*To love and
be loved*

Orange

Your strength is skillfulness! If your brightest color is orange, you need freedom to take immediate action! A zest for life and a desire to test the limits best express your nature. You take pride in being highly skilled in a variety of fields.

You are a master negotiator. Adventure is your middle name. You prefer a hands-on approach to problem-solving, and a direct line of reasoning creates the excitement and immediate results that you admire.

Your Keys To Personal Success:

The impulse to really live	Testing the limits
The need for variation	Excitement and lightheartedness
Charged adventure	Being a natural entertainer
Spontaneous relationships	Taking off for somewhere else
Being able to act in a crisis	A love of tools
Charm, wit, and fun	Taking defeats only temporarily
Consider waiting an emotional death	

You Tend To:

Dream of:	Being free, spontaneity, and impetuousness
Value:	Skills, grace, finesse, and charisma
Regard:	Opportunities, options, and competition
Dislike:	Rigidness, authority, and forcelessness
Express:	Optimism, impatience, eagerness, and confidence
Foster:	Recreation, fun, and enjoyment
Respect:	Skill and artistic expression

True Colors

Where's the action?

Gold

Your strength is duty! If your brightest color is gold, you value order and cherish the traditions of home and family. You provide for and support the structure of society. Steadfastness and loyalty are your trademarks.

Generous and parental by nature, you show you care by making everyone do the right thing. To disregard responsibility of any kind never occurs to you.

Your Keys To Personal Success:

Generosity	The work ethic
A parental nature	Ceremony
A sense of history	Dignity, culture
Perpetuating heritage	Steadfastness
A value of order	Predictability
Home and family	Establishing and organizing institutions

You Tend To:

Dream of:	Assets, wealth, influence, status, and security
Value:	Dependability, accountability, and responsibility
Regard:	Service and dedication
Dislike:	Disobedience, non-conformity, and insubordination
Express:	Concern, stability, and purpose
Foster:	Institutions and traditions
Respect:	Loyalty and obligation
Promote:	Groups, ties, bonds, associations, and organizations

True Colors

Plan it!

The 4 personal styles

PERSONAL STYLE	BLUE	GREEN	GOLD	ORANGE
core need	self-actualization	competency	social belonging	freedom
overall mood	enthusiasm	cool, calm, collected	concerned	excitable
trust	imagination	logic, consistency	authority	chance
pride themselves for	empathy	competence	dependability	impact
in management	the catalyst	the visionary	the traditionalist	the troubleshooter
perception	significance	categorical	discrepancy	harmonics
supports, fosters	growth	invention	institutions	recreation
virtue	loyalty	strength, determination	generosity	courage
stressed by	feeling artificial	inadequate	rejection	restrictions, rigidity
strives for, seeks	love	insight	jurisdiction	freedom
at work	a catalyst, harmonizing	pragmatic	procedural	varied
esteemed by	helping people	finding insights	being of service	being resourceful
wants to be appreciated for	unique contributions	ideas	accuracy, thoroughness	cleverness
intrinsic intelligence	with people	with strategy	with material	with senses
when disturbed	becomes hysterical	becomes compulsive	becomes complaining	becomes punitive
searching for	roles	problems	security	stimulation
dislikes	hypocrisy	injustice	disobedience	ineptness, clumsiness
thinks	dogmatically	agnostically	pessimistically	opportunistically

True Colors

The 4 personal styles continued . . .

PERSONAL STYLE	BLUE	GREEN	GOLD	ORANGE
fantasizes being	a messiah	a wizard, genius	an aristocrat	a virtuoso
loves	integrity, honesty	justice	obedience	grace, elegance
causes guilt	letting someone down	lacking will power	greed	cowardice
irritated by	being treated impersonally	illogical thinking	violating rules and regulations	being told how to do things
mood in relationships	meaningful	aloof, objective	serious, responsible	sensuous, exciting
rewarded by	acceptance of who they are	affirming their wisdom	appreciating their service	being given freedom
nurtures	vision of a better world	technological insights	helpfulness	competitiveness

Exercise 2

Autograph signing

Sign your name in your preferred hand (the hand you usually write with).

Now sign your name in your non-preferred hand (the other hand).

What was your experience when you wrote with your:

preferred hand?:

non-preferred hand?:

Just as you have a preference for one hand, you also have preferences for certain personality characteristics.

Exercise 3

My color preferences

Why I think _____ is my first color

_____

_____

_____

_____

_____

Why I think _____ is my second color

_____

_____

_____

_____

_____

_____

_____

Why I think _____ is my third color

_____

_____

_____

_____

_____

_____

_____

_____

True Colors

Why I think _____ is my fourth color

_____

_____

_____

_____

_____

_____

_____

Are you more extroverted or introverted?

Extroverts:
- usually relate more to their outer world of people and things than to their inner world of ideas.
- are often good at greeting people
- usually communicate well
- often don't mind being interrupted by answering the telephone.
- usually like having people around them

Introverts:
- usually relate more easily to their inner world of ideas than to their outer world of people and things.
- prefer quiet for concentration
- sometimes have problems communicating
- usually dislike telephone interruptions
- like to work alone

True Colors

Exercise 4

Extroverted or introverted?

Discuss whether you are introverted, extroverted, or somewhere in between.

I consider myself to be more _____ than _____ because

_____

_____

_____

_____

_____

Or

I believe I am somewhere in between the two extremes because

_____

_____

_____

_____

Your Role Versus Your Identity

People often confuse the roles—student, sister, brother, parent, employee— they play in life with their identity. Your identity is who you are. It determines how you will naturally behave in a particular role, but the role does not change who you are.

Exercise 5

Roles I play

Describe three roles you play. Are you expressing your true self in each one?

Role #1_____

Description

_____

_____

I do or do not feel like I express my true self in this role because

_____

_____

Role #2_____

Description

_____

_____

I do or do not feel like I express my true self in this role because

_____

_____

True Colors

Role #3_____

Description

_____

_____

I do or do not feel like I express my true self in this role because

_____

_____

_____

Exercise 6

A successful role

Imagine and describe yourself in a successful role that you would like to play.

_____

_____

_____

_____

_____

_____

_____

True Colors

What personality characteristics do you express in this role?

_____

_____

_____

_____

_____

_____

What would have to change in your life for you to play this ideal role?

_____

_____

_____

_____

_____

_____

True Colors

Chapter 3

Short Journal (5 minutes or less)

What I have learned about myself in this chapter is:

_____

_____

_____

_____

_____

_____

_____

_____

_____

_____

_____

_____

_____

_____

_____

True Colors

True Colors

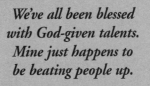

*We've all been blessed
with God-given talents.
Mine just happens to
be beating people up.*

— Sugar Ray Leaonard
Championship Boxer

Chapter
4

CLUES TO
YOUR HIDDEN
TALENTS

Chapter 4

Clues to Your Hidden Talents

There are 2 clues to discovering your hidden talents—clues that will reveal your natural strengths. Let's look at the first clue: identifying your true values. In the process of choosing or changing careers, it is important to clarify your beliefs. Values are at the core of beliefs and they can be anything you regard highly—ideas, activities, and things that you prize. If you observe your own activities, you will be able to identify your values because values are what you do, not necessarily what you say.

Because a person has a variety of alternatives on the basis of what he or she values, a clarification of values is extremely crucial to every part of the career decision-making process. If values are not clearly defined, the method of achieving them and the degree of their realization will also be unclear.

True Values

Exercise 1

A talent is both a gift and obligation.

Values and the Four Primary Colors

In line with personality preferences, those things you value are consistent with your temperament. Blue values differ from gold, green, and orange values. By acknowledging your preferences, you will better understand your own values. Circle the values that you relate to in each color group.

It's nice to be important, but it's more important to be nice.

Blue True Values
Authenticity
Being acknowledged
Communication
Compassion
Creativity
Democracy
Emotions
Empathy

Enthusiasm
Friendship
Harmony
Honesty
Individuality
Integrity
Intuition
Love
Natural potential
Optimism
Patience
Peace
Pleasing others
Positive feedback
Public contact
Relationships
Romance
Self-understanding
Sensitivity
Sincerity
Spirituality
Tact
Teamwork
Trustworthiness
Unity

Green True Values

Circle the values that you relate to.

Abstraction
Autonomy
Brevity
Cleverness
Competence
Cool-headed under pressure
Creativity
Curiosity

Money can't buy love.

A problem is a chance for you to do your best.
— Duke Ellington

Ethics
Fairness
Focus
Future orientation
Ideas
Imagination
Independence
Ingenuity
Invention
Innovation
Intelligence
Knowledge
Logic
Mental challenge
Objectivity
Precise language
Privacy
Power
Rationality
Self-confidence
Theory
Truth
Vision
Wisdom

Gold True Values

Circle the values that you relate to.

Accuracy
Achievement
Affiliation
Authority
Being meticulous
Caution
Community
Compensation
Completion

If A equals success, then the formula is A equals X plus Y plus Z, where X is work, Y is play, Z is keep your mouth shut

Is life worth living? This is a question for an embryo, not a man.

— Samuel Butler

TrueColors

Hard work without talent is a shame, but talent without hard work is a tragedy.

— Robert Half

Conformity
Cooperation
Decisiveness
Dependability
Duty
Efficiency
Facts and data
Family
Justice
Loyalty
Morality
Orderliness
Predictability
Prestige
Profit
Punctuality
Recognition
Religion
Respect
Responsibility
Routine
Rules
Safety
Security
Service
Stability
Status
Structure
Tradition
Wealth

Orange True Values

Circle the values that you relate to.

Action and activity
Adventure
Aesthetics

The only way to enjoy anything in life is to earn it first.

Affluence means influence.

— Jack London

True Colors

Life is ours to be spent, not to be saved.

— D. H. Lawrence

Artistic creativity
Camaraderie
Change
Competition
Energy
Entertainment
Excitement
Fast pace
Flexibility
Freedom
Fun
Generosity
Humor
Independence
Optimism
Physical challenge
Playfulness
Pleasure
Profit
Skillfulness
Spontaneity
Variety

Exercise 2

Prioritizing your values

How many values did you circle in each color group?

Blue   _____

Green   _____

Gold   _____

Orange   _____

True Colors

*It is better to
live rich than
to die rich.*

— Samuel Johnson

Are the totals consistent with the order of your test results? Why or why not?

_____

_____

_____

_____

_____

_____

Exercise 3

Experiencing your values

Our values show through events that happen in our lives. Write about two major life experiences or events that you remember as being special to you.

Major life experience #1

_____

_____

_____

_____

_____

True Colors

Which values were you demonstrating?

_____

_____

_____

_____

Major life experience #2

_____

_____

_____

_____

_____

_____

_____

True Colors

Which values were you demonstrating?

_____

_____

_____

_____

Exercise 4

Values Questionnaire

By answering the following questions, you will be able to recognize some of your values.

1. On what have you spent most of your money?

_____

_____

_____

What values can you recognize?

_____

_____

2. Describe a major decision that has made you happy.

_____

_____

_____

What values can you recognize?

_____

_____

True Colors

3. What is your favorite activity?

_____

_____

What values can you recognize?

_____

_____

4. What would you consider an ideal vacation?

_____

_____

What values can you recognize?

_____

_____

Who are your role models? Name three and briefly discuss what they have in common with you.

1. _____

_____

2. _____

_____

3. _____

_____

What values can you recognize?

_____

_____

Exercise 5

Hobbies

A career may not meet all of your values, but the more of them you meet, the more satisfied you will be. Ensure that your additional values are being satisfied through some area of your life; hobbies are a good outlet for expressing values. List any hobbies you might have.

1.

2.

3.

4.

5.

What values do you recognize through your hobbies?

1.

2.

3.

4.

5.

6.

7.

8.

9.

10.

Exercise 6

Visualize your work environment

Answer these questions to visualize your ideal work environment.

1. Are you working indoors or outdoors?

2. Are you located in one place or are you traveling from one place to another?

3. Do you work alone or with others?

4. Are you working with children or adults?

5. What are you doing that gives you satisfaction?

Think of careers that correspond to this experience and list them below:

1.

2.

3.

4.

5.

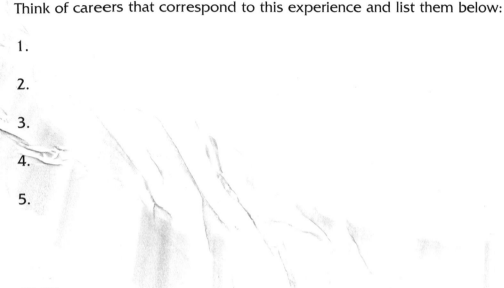

Skills

Natural gifts and talents & the 4 primary colors

We've established that the first clue to discovering your hidden talents is to identify your true values. Now let's look at the second clue: identifying what you enjoy doing.

We all have an abundance of skills. The question is, which of these skills do we prefer to use in a career? Again, using personality preferences, we can focus on the skills we use naturally and have developed because of preference. An example would be writing with your dominant or preferred hand. You can write with both hands, but you probably write much better with one than the other. When you write with the hand that is dominant, you will do it without struggling and it will flow much better. The same is true when you use your unique gifts and talents. You will experience ease and comfort and therefore, using these skills will seem natural and more enjoyable.

Skills listed in the following color groups are the natural gifts and talents for the corresponding personality.

Blue skills

Natural gifts & talents

Your natural gifts are things that you are good at and enjoy doing. Notice how many of these skills involve helping other people, yet they are not specific to only one type of work. These are your transferable skills, which can be used in many diverse occupations. These skills will help you identify work that will give you a sense of passion and fulfillment. Put a star next to the skills you most prefer to use.

Acknowledging others - recognizing and validating others for who they are

Building rapport - bringing harmony to a relationship

Building self-esteem - helping others feel good about themselves

Communicating - effectively exchanging verbal or written information with others

Consulting - giving professional advice

Coordinating - bringing people and activities together in a harmonious way

Counseling - helping others with their personal and professional problems

Enlightening - giving spiritual insight

Expressing feelings - openly communicating feelings with other people

Facilitating groups - assisting a group to harmoniously move in a positive positive direction

Fostering - nurturing

Guiding others - steering or directing people in a positive direction

Healing - restoring health

Make Love, not war.

Sometimes give your service for nothing . . .
— Hippocrates

Helping others - improving the lives of others

Influencing others - having an effect on the lives of other people

Inspiring others - having an exalting influence upon others

Interviewing others - using good communication skills to obtain information from another person

Leading - acting as a positive role model more than being in a position of power or authority

Listening - hearing and paying attention to what others have to say

Mentoring - coaching and supporting others in the direction they want to go in

Motivating - acting as a catalyst to move others to action

Nurturing - developing and fostering the potential in others

Public speaking - effectively using language to make speeches in public

Recruiting - getting others involved in whatever they believe in

Supporting others - assisting others emotionally

Teaching - enlightening others and motivating them to learn

Training - directing the growth of others

Visualizing - imagining possibilities

Working as a team - bringing a group together to meet a common goal

True Colors

Green skills

Natural gifts & talents

Your natural gifts are things that you are good at and enjoy doing. Notice the emphasis on mental activity, but these skills are not specific to only one type of work. These are your transferable skills, which can be used in many diverse occupations. These skills will help you identify work that will give you a sense of passion and fulfillment. Put a star next to the skills you most prefer to use.

Analyzing - separating or distinguishing the component parts of something to as to discover its true nature or inner relationships

Conceptualizing - forming abstract ideas in the mind

Consulting - giving technical information or providing ideas to define, clarify or sharpen procedures, capabilities, or product specifications

Critiquing - analyzing, evaluating, or appreciating works of art

Curing - restoring to health after a disease

Debating - discussing a question by considering opposing arguments

Designing - mentally conceiving and planning

Developing - making something available to improve a situation

Diagnosing - analyzing the cause or nature of a condition, situation, or problem

Editing - improving and directing publications

Generating ideas - brainstorming or dreaming up ideas

Intellectualizing - using the intellect rather than emotion or experience

Interpreting ideas - explaining the meaning of ideas

The successful people are the ones who think up things for the rest of the world to keep busy at.

— Don Marquis

True Colors

There may now exist great men for things that do not exist.

— Samuel Burchardt

Inventing - developing or creating something for the first time

Learning - gaining knowledge

Observing - examining people, data or things scientifically

Problem solving - identifying key issues or factors in a problem, generating ideas and solutions to solve the problem, selecting the best approach, and testing and evaluating it

Proofreading - reading and marking corrections

Reasoning - thinking

Researching - investigating and experimenting aimed at the discovery and interpretation of facts

Synthesizing - integrating ideas and information

Thinking logically - subjecting ideas to the process of logical thought

Writing - expressing by means of words

Gold skills

Natural gifts & talents

Your natural gifts are things that you are good at and enjoy doing. Notice the emphasis on implementation, but these skills are not specific to only one type of work. These are your transferable skills, which can be used in many diverse occupations. These skills will help you identify work that will give you a sense of passion and fulfillment. Put a star next to the skills you most prefer to use.

Administering policies - managing a course or method of action

Allocating resources - designating resources for a specific purpose

True Colors

If at first you don't succeed, try reading the instructions.

Attending to detail - paying attention to small items

Bookkeeping - recording the accounts or transactions of a business

Budgeting - planning the amount of money that is available for, required for, or assigned to a particular purpose

Calculating - determining by mathematical means

Caretaking - taking care of the physical needs of others, especially children, the sick and the elderly

Collecting data - gathering information

Coordinating - taking care of logistics for events to flow smoothly

Decision-making - bringing things to a conclusion

Delegating - entrusting responsibilities to other people

Dispatching - sending off or away with promptness

Establishing procedures - constructing a series of steps to be followed in accomplishing something

Estimating cost - judging approximately the value or worth of something

Evaluating - appraising the worth, significance or status of something

Following directions - doing specifically the things told to do by others verbally or in writing

Following through - completing an activity planned or begun

Guarding - protecting or defending

Maintaining schedules - overseeing something designated for a fixed, future time

Maintaining records - accurate and up-to-date record-keeping

True Colors

Managing - directing or conducting business or affairs

Monitoring - watching, observing, or checking for a specific purpose

Organizing - arranging things in a systematic order

Paying attention to detail - looking for smaller elements

Planning - making a way of proceeding

Preparing - getting something ready for use or getting ready for some occasion

Recording - putting things in writing

Regulating - governing or directing according to rule or law

Securing - relieving from exposure to danger

Serving - making a contribution to the welfare of others

Supervising - taking responsibility for the work done by others

Orange skills

Natural gifts & talents

Your natural gifts are things that you are good at and enjoy doing. Notice the emphasis on activity, but these skills are not specific to only one type of work. These are your transferable skills, which can be used in many diverse occupations. These skills will help you identify work that will give you a sense of passion and fulfillment. Put a star next to the skills you most prefer to use.

Assembling things - fitting together the parts of things

Coaching - training intensively by instruction, demonstration, and practice

Either lead, follow, or get out of the way.

— Sign on desk of Ted Turner

Competing - challenging another for the purpose of winning

Constructing - building something

Dancing - performing rhythmic and patterned bodily movements, usually to music

Displaying things - arranging something in an eye-catching exhibit

Drafting - drawing the preliminary sketch, version, or plan for something

Entertaining - performing publicly for amusement

Gardening - cultivating a plot of ground with herbs, fruits, flowers or vegetables

Illustrating - providing visual features intended to explain or decorate

Influencing others - causing an effect on others

Manipulating - treating or operating with the hands or by mechanical means

Manufacturing - making from raw materials by hand or by machinery

Marketing - planning and strategizing how to present a product or service in the marketplace

Negotiating - conferring with another so as to arrive at the settlement of some matter

Operating tools - skillfully handling tools to perform work

Operating vehicles - driving cabs, limousines, heavy equipment, etc.

Performing - practicing an art that involves public performance

Persuading - influencing others in favor of a product, service, or point of view

Promoting - persuading people to see the value of an idea, person, activity, or cause

Public speaking - expressing yourself before a group

Repairing - restoring by replacing a part or putting together what is torn or broken

Responding to emergencies - being spontaneous and level-headed in emergency situations

Risk taking - having a dangerous element to life

Selling - promoting a service or product with the intent of getting someone to buy or accept it in exchange for something, usually money

Exercise 7

Job skills

Read through the sample job description below and underline the skills used by a Career Counselor.

Position Title: Career Counselor

Description of duties and responsibilities: Career or vocational counselors help people define their lifestyle, identify skills and aptitudes, develop job hunting skills, select satisfying work and leisure activities. Career counselors use discussion, exercises and tests to determine the client's personality, abilities, interests and values. Then they assist the client in gathering information about career options, evaluating the options, selecting a goal and defining the steps to be taken to reach the goal. They work with clients individually, in groups or in classes. They may keep records of the clients they work with and they must continually keep up with changes in the labor market and be aware of new counseling techniques. They may also help clients write resumes, prepare for interviews and coach them through the job search process. In large companies they may explain career paths or company transfer policies and procedures.

Exercise 8

Create your own job description:

Forget about job titles for a minute. Imagine your ideal occupation/work setting, then write your own job description. Be sure to include the nature of the work: job duties, amount of education or training required, which skills you want to use, the salary and benefits you want, and other important qualities. Make sure you include what you want to spend your day doing and how you want to express yourself.

_____

_____

_____

_____

_____

_____

_____

_____

_____

_____

_____

Underline your true values and skills included in your job description.

Exercise 9

Achievements

Now choose two achievements that you are particularly proud of and write a paragraph for each, identifying which skills you were using. Do these skills match the skills listed in your color group?

Achievement #1

_____

_____

_____

_____

_____

_____

Underline skills used.

Which are consistent with your color group?

_____

_____

_____

_____

_____

True Colors

Luck is not something you can mention in the presence of self-made men.

— F. B. White

Achievement #2

_____

_____

_____

_____

_____

_____

_____

Underline the skills used.

Which are consistent with your color group?

_____

_____

_____

_____

_____

_____

_____

True Colors

Exercise 10

How do you see me?

Ask another person to describe you. Write their description below.

_____

_____

_____

_____

_____

_____

_____

_____

_____

_____

How is the way that person described you different from how you see yourself? Why?

_____

_____

_____

True Colors

What insights have you gained?

True Colors

LEADERSHIP STYLES

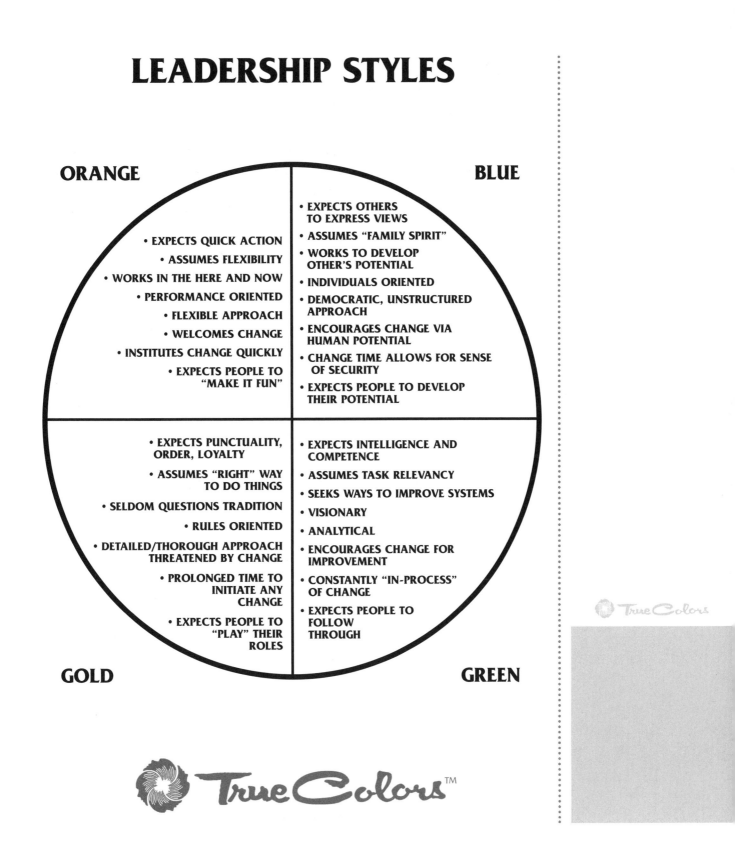

ORANGE

- EXPECTS QUICK ACTION
- ASSUMES FLEXIBILITY
- WORKS IN THE HERE AND NOW
- PERFORMANCE ORIENTED
- FLEXIBLE APPROACH
- WELCOMES CHANGE
- INSTITUTES CHANGE QUICKLY
- EXPECTS PEOPLE TO "MAKE IT FUN"

BLUE

- EXPECTS OTHERS TO EXPRESS VIEWS
- ASSUMES "FAMILY SPIRIT"
- WORKS TO DEVELOP OTHER'S POTENTIAL
- INDIVIDUALS ORIENTED
- DEMOCRATIC, UNSTRUCTURED APPROACH
- ENCOURAGES CHANGE VIA HUMAN POTENTIAL
- CHANGE TIME ALLOWS FOR SENSE OF SECURITY
- EXPECTS PEOPLE TO DEVELOP THEIR POTENTIAL

GOLD

- EXPECTS PUNCTUALITY, ORDER, LOYALTY
- ASSUMES "RIGHT" WAY TO DO THINGS
- SELDOM QUESTIONS TRADITION
- RULES ORIENTED
- DETAILED/THOROUGH APPROACH THREATENED BY CHANGE
- PROLONGED TIME TO INITIATE ANY CHANGE
- EXPECTS PEOPLE TO "PLAY" THEIR ROLES

GREEN

- EXPECTS INTELLIGENCE AND COMPETENCE
- ASSUMES TASK RELEVANCY
- SEEKS WAYS TO IMPROVE SYSTEMS
- VISIONARY
- ANALYTICAL
- ENCOURAGES CHANGE FOR IMPROVEMENT
- CONSTANTLY "IN-PROCESS" OF CHANGE
- EXPECTS PEOPLE TO FOLLOW THROUGH

True Colors™

Exercise 11

What kind of leader am I?

Each personality is capable of being a leader, but their style will be different. Your success depends on how consistent your style is with your natural strengths. The leadership styles diagram on the previous page shows how each color prefers to lead. Write a paragraph discussing a time when you were a leader.

_____

_____

_____

_____

_____

_____

_____

_____

_____

_____

_____

_____

_____

True Colors

Judge a leader by the followers.

Explain how the statements on the diagram describe your leadership style in this example.

_____

_____

_____

_____

_____

_____

_____

Exercise 12

Post-test

My first color represents my major strengths, the things I do well.
My strengths are:

1.

2.

3.

4.

5.

6.

True Colors

7.

8.

9.

10.

My last color represents my weaknesses, the things I do not do as well. My weaknesses are:

1.

2.

3.

4.

5.

6.

7.

8.

9.

10.

True Colors

Capitalize on your strengths; they are most important to use in your work. Know what you are good at and focus on those areas. Also, understand your weaknesses in order to manage them. Improve these areas as needed, but with less emphasis on them in the workplace.

Chapter 4

Short Journal (5 minutes or less)

Your personal strengths are revealed through your values and natural gifts and talents. Describe the difference between your lists of strengths on the pre-test in chapter 1, exercise 1, and what you have discovered about your unique strengths.

_____

_____

_____

_____

_____

_____

_____

_____

_____

_____

_____

_____

True Colors

*Men are created different,
they lose their social
freedom and their individual
autonomy in seeking
to become like each other.*
— David Reisman

Chapter 5

SELF-ESTEEM

Chapter 5

Self-Esteem

Self-esteem is an inside job. It is intrinsic and as natural as breathing. You do not need to do anything other than be who you are to feel good about yourself. You already have what it takes to experience self-esteem, and it belongs to you as your human right.

We have been lead to believe that if we have all the material success we desire, we will feel good about ourselves. In reality, the opposite is true. We only need to be who we are and do what we love in order to have what we desire. If we feel good about ourselves we can have all of those other things. That is why it is so difficult for some people to achieve success—they are doing things in the reverse.

Our self-perceptions drive us in a direction toward success or in a direction away from it. Our natural strengths are our built-in program for self-esteem and success, and it is with these unique gifts and talents that we will begin our examination of career decision-making.

This chapter, as well as subsequent ones, will give you the knowledge you require to begin the road to high self-esteem and success.

Self-Esteeming Characteristics by Color Group

Let's take a look at the self-esteem characteristics manifest in the four primary color groups.

Green: The Need To Be Ingenious.

As a green, you are in esteem when you feel competent. You want to understand and control the realities of life. This control represents the power to acquire the multiple abilities for which you pride yourself.

You feel best about yourself when you are solving problems and when your ideas are recognized. You are a complex individualist with great analytical ability. Although you do not express you emotions openly, you do experience deep feelings.

A man possesses talent; genius possesses the man.

— Issac Stern

An abstract thinker, you are symbolized by the vision of the genius; the challenge of science; the complexity of models and systems; and in the perfection of symmetry, such as that demonstrated in the great Pyramids.

You thrive on your mental competencies as well as on the skills and abilities of others. You are motivated by a quest for knowledge and the ability to seek it and provide it. The control of knowledge is as important as its acquisition because such control can be perceived as power.

You are motivated to improve

The performance aspect of knowledge is not of primary concern. You prefer, rather, to provide information for others to act upon. From those results, you are motivated even further to improve on that which you have previously perceived or created. The importance and emphasis on performance concerns you only when it is your own, as with the development of an idea or the pursuit of new knowledge.

Language as a communication tool

The Green personality seeks gratification in professions which rely on competence, including the sciences, engineering, computers and mathematics, philosophy, and any field which requires precise detailing of ideas. Language and its use are merely toys with which to play; you have a certain fascination with language as a communication tool.

Relationships on an intellectual level

Relationships you establish with others may appear to be only on an intellectual level. This tends to cause others to be unfeeling and distant. Your enthusiasm in directing attention only to those with whom you share a mental rapport is seen as withholding thoughts and emotions from others.

Working as a source of pleasure

As a Green, you derive genuine pleasure from work because it represents a continual quest for knowledge. Work is the means of providing creature comforts and also a source of recreation. On any day away from your regular work, you are content to sit before the television and listen only to informational programs. To be mentally idle is to be worthless.

Detaching to determine the "why"

Because you often detach or step back to reflect the "why" of your experi-

True Colors

If ignorance is bliss, why aren't more people happy?

ences, that detachment may prevent you from having the experience yourself. You may feel that the experience itself may not be required to comprehend it.

Blue: The Need To Be Authentic.

As a Blue, you are in esteem when you are authentic. You must find your real self and live your life as an expression of your unique identity. Integrity means unity of inner self with outer expression.

Life is a dream in which you must find meaning. You are sensitive to subtlety and create roles - with special flair - in life's drama. You enjoy close relationships with those you love and experience a spiritual pride in your nature. Making a difference in the world comes easily as you cultivate the potential in yourself and in others.

A natural harmonizer, you are symbolized by the vision of peace; the romance of love ballads; the drama of stage and screen; the importance of people; and the warmth of a hug and a handshake.

The exclusive Blue segment maintains a powerful influence over the rest of society, in that so many creative writers belong to this color grouping. Journalists, poets, playwrights, novelists, and biographers who are generally motivated to inspire others are nearly exclusively of the Blue personality type.

Continuing the search for self

From childhood, the enigmatic and continual search for self began and continues to this day. Human relationships are of primary concern to you, not only on a one-on-one basis, but among the people of the world, as well. You often behave with almost chameleon ability to preserve a personal relationship. You even will be that which others want you to be in order to provide an atmosphere of harmony. You explore and consume new directions, ideas, and conceptions dealing with human relationships. You romanticize your own experiences and those of others in an effort to bring importance to the energy expended.

Relating on a personal level

You relate best to others on a personal level. This leads you into professions such as psychology, counseling, teaching, social work, and the ministry.

True Colors

You are not in competition with anyone but yourself

Communication is such a part of your life that in these professions you are able to express your concerns with poetic license and with flair. You treat your work almost in a missionary sense, with the emphasis on those benefits that will be derived rather than on the job itself. You devote more time than any other color group to developing this personal aspect because you seek the same fulfillment for yourself that you attempt to give to others.

Seeking identity through contribution
You seek identity through contribution. The significance of the contribution need not bring personal acknowledgment, and in many cases you receive fewer rewards than do all other color groups. But you continue to pursue those esoteric goals which you feel are neglected by society.

Seeing things through to the end
Time is not captive to you. When involved in a meaningful personal relationship or working on a project which requires an inordinate amount of time, you have a compulsion to see it through to the end. You consider the time well spent, not only as a benefit to yourself, but because you feel that if you could not provide the attention, it would probably not be provided by others.

Tapping into universal harmony
You enjoy a natural affinity with nature and with all phenomena of the human experience. You attempt to tap into what you perceive to be the harmony of the universe in all that you do and experience.

Orange: The Need To Be Skillful

As an Orange, you are in esteem when, above all, you are free to act on a moment's notice. You choose to be impulsive and act upon the idea of the moment. Action or doing carries its own reward.

Adventure is your middle name, and you do things for the joy of doing. A zest for life and a desire to test the limits exemplify your Orange personality. You take pride in being highly skilled in a variety of fields, and are a master negotiator. Your hands-on approach to problem solving and direct line of reasoning creates excitement and immediate results.

This free spirit is symbolized by the flight of an eagle; the sensation of

Anything you're good at contributes to happiness.
— Bertrand Russel

True Colors

It is better to die on your feet than to live on your knees.
— Delores Ibarruri

hang-gliding; the action and risk of driving a motorcycle; the skillfulness of handling a tool; and the freedom of the out-of-doors.

Your Orange personality's zest for action and freedom are as much a part of the culture of this country as are the tradition and duty of the Gold personality.

Acting on impulse

You thrive on being able to act on impulse—to be expressive without reluctance. Professions which intrigue and excite you include the world of entertainment, athletics, and those art forms which demand skill, such as photography, dance, and music. Orange personality types are also attracted to law enforcement. It is the passion which accompanies skill that provides lure for the Orange.

Enjoying new ideas and goals

Life to the Orange is a series of new situations, new ideas, and new goals. Rules are recognized, but broken if necessary. You enjoy owning tools, gadgets, or anything representing newer, faster, and better methods to accomplish a goal. Keeping things on an even keel is not your strong suit. Change, to you, is not only exciting, but often preferable.

Being with people

You enjoy being with people and are often the recognized leader. You easily run interference for others, relishing an opportunity to reflect the importance of doing so. You generate a genuine camaraderie with others using your gregarious nature to evoke trust from them.

Dealing with pressure

You deal with pressure and physical demands far more easily than do other color groups. The adage, "no pain, no gain," is a byword for you. That kind of stamina provides the backdrop for your competitive nature, a nature from which you derive pleasure. This competitiveness also means that you will achieve goals with perfection.

Being misunderstood

Orange types are at times perceived to be less than sensitive to others. You are often misunderstood in your drive to accomplish something with only the end result in mind. While others may be charmed by your ability and enthusiasm, they can also become confused by your unorthodox methods.

True Colors

Acting without reservation

Freedom is your ultimate pleasure—freedom to act without reservation, to make decisions without approval or obligation. You enjoy boundless energy which you believe should be used to its highest potential. Life is an adventure and you believe you know exactly how to make the best of it.

Gold: The Need To Be Responsible

As a Gold, you are in esteem when you feel responsible and belong to a social unit. Regardless of which social unit is involved, you feel you must earn your place of belonging by being useful, fulfilling responsibilities, being of service, and caring for others.

Steadfastness and loyalty are your trademarks; you value order and cherish traditions of home and family. You are generous and parental, demonstrating that you care by ensuring that everyone does the right thing.

The backbones of society, Golds are symbolized in the patriotism of the American flag; the structure of groups and organizations; the security of banks and savings books; the responsibility of parenting; the caring of nursing and healing; and the pride of lineage and aristocracy.

From the moment your personality began to develop, a sense of obligation and duty also began to emerge. Rules by which people interact are of utmost concern to you. Security of the family unit and for all it stands is the foundation by which all other interactions are expressed, be it in the school, the workplace, the church, social units, or society itself.

Finding comfort in structure

Examples of the Gold structure are edified early in life. Organizations such as the Boy Scouts and Girl Scouts are the groundwork for the future comfort zones of Golds. You are drawn to service organizations, making the time spent in these activities almost your recreation. To be part of an organization makes you feel as if you are the organization; titles, banners, flags, and similar forms of identification are necessary symbols representing the physical stamps of approval for your behavior.

Enjoying responsibility

For you, responsibility is a blessing. You are the premier conservator on con-

Liberty means responsibility. That is why most men dread it.

— Antonio de Mendoza

tinuity and perpetuity. Even the apparent "dumping" on you of those duties others will not perform cannot dissuade you from your continuing quest for responsibility.

Providing standards to society

You have a distinct concern for others, which differs from that of a Blue personality. Your concern is to provide standards within the society to better enable people to tend to obligations. The financial world is the domain of the Gold. Education, medicine, and service occupations are all areas to which you are drawn.

Revering history

You have a reverence for history and its importance, and from this you develop a background for stability and the perpetuity of institutions. Change represents a threat to you. Social change must come slowly and methodically, and in the workplace changes must come only after research and cooperation. You do not support revolutionary changes or those that appear to be merely "Band-Aid" or quick fixes.

Establishing stability

Your sense of duty comes from having established stability and strength in your life pattern. You express yourself with concrete examples of your Gold personality, be it with your family, home, job, or social activities. These represent your basic motivation and direction, and society esteems you because you exemplify that which society itself strives to accomplish.

Exercise 1

What makes me feel good?

As a _____ person, I have learned that what makes me feel good about myself is

_____

_____

_____

True Colors

_____

_____

_____

_____

_____

_____

_____

_____

Exercise 2

Expressing self-esteem

Understanding yourself and the ways in which you relate to the world will provide opportunities to expand you perspectives. Most importantly, once you recognize those characteristics that are esteeming, you will also develop a compassion for people different than yourself.

Write a brief story about something you have done that made you feel really good about yourself. Take special note of which characteristics from your color key are expressed in the story you relate.

_____

_____

_____

True Colors

Self-actualization

Self-actualization is our highest need. We all want to express our true selves and reach our potential, and pursuing your ideal career is a means to doing just that. How you choose to self-actualize is the key. Each color is motivated to do this in a different way. The chart below demonstrates how the four personalities choose to reach their potential through self-actualization.

The Four Paths to Self-actualization

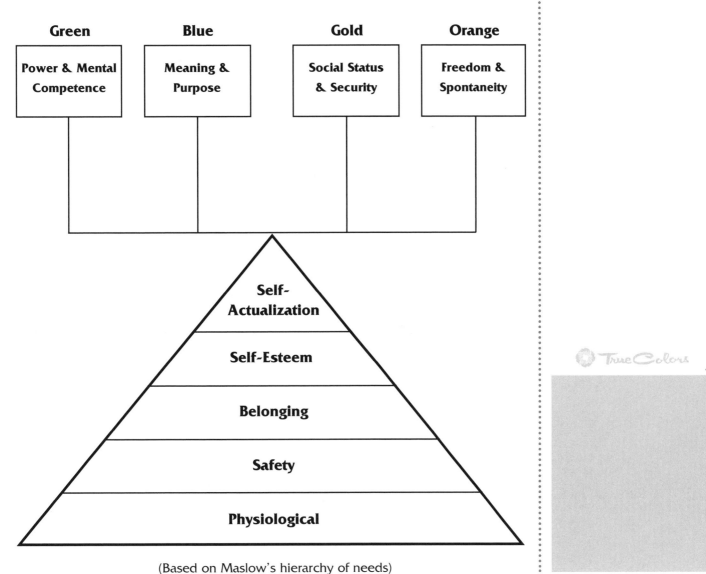

Green	Blue	Gold	Orange
Power & Mental Competence	Meaning & Purpose	Social Status & Security	Freedom & Spontaneity

Self-Actualization

Self-Esteem

Belonging

Safety

Physiological

(Based on Maslow's hierarchy of needs)

Exercise 3

Expressing your best self

Choose your primary color below, then give an example of when you have felt self-actualized.

If your first color is:

Green
When have you experienced being powerful or mentally competent?

_____

_____

_____

_____

Blue
When have you experienced feeling meaning and purpose in your life?

_____

_____

_____

_____

Orange
When have you experienced being free and spontaneous?

_____

True Colors

_____

_____

_____

Gold

When have you experienced having social status and security in your life?

_____

_____

_____

Exercise 4

What Causes You Stress?

Write a one-minute essay about those things that cause stress in your life.

_____

_____

_____

_____

_____

_____

_____

_____

_____

_____

_____

_____

_____

_____

_____

_____

_____

_____

Things That Cause Stress for Greens

Too many rules
People who get in the way of executing strategy
Incompetence in self or others
Control
Disorganization of system
Rigidity
People who don't value knowledge and learning
Lack of freedom
Not knowing
Off-task distraction

Unfairness
Committee meetings that have no point
Unreasonable emotional outbursts
Labels
No new horizons
Policy and procedures
Welfare mindset
Schedules that make no sense
Stupid people

Things That Cause Stress for Blues

Disharmony
Judgmental people
Lack of communication
Chaos
Injustice
Rigidity
Isolation
Overly aggressive people
Paperwork and too many details
Cruelty to children and animals
Being yelled at
Being lied to
Conflict
Tunnel vision
Procedures/red tape
Politics
Bossy, negative people
Arrogance
Lack of support
Narrow-mindedness
Lack of understanding
No hugs
Heartlessness
Lack of integrity
Insensitivity
Not being able to express oneself

Lack of romance
Cynics
People who won't grow
Dealing with untrustworthy people
Unresolved confrontations

Things That Cause Stress for Golds

Inefficiency
Lack of order
Flaky people
Unreliable people
People who are late
Lack of leadership
Non-cooperation
Not knowing what is expected
Slobs
Procrastinators
Waiting
Loud people
Disorganized people
Being told what to do by others
Change
Inconsistency
Things not working out like they think they should
Can't get things done "right"
Not belonging
Lack of control

Things That Cause Stress for Oranges

Boredom
Being on time
Unnecessary routine
Deadlines
Lack of humor
Slow people

Lack of money
Car problems
Paperwork
Bureaucracy
Lack of sex
Criticism
Negativity
Nagging
Inflexibility
Unbending rules
Schedules
Waiting
Sameness
Predictability
Traffic

Exercise 5

Stress in my life

Are some of the stressors you wrote about in exercise 4 listed for your color?
List other stressors you did not write about.

1.

2.

3.

4.

5.

Stress can lead to out-of-esteem behavior. We are always striving to feel good about ourselves, but when it can't be done in a positive way it will be done in any way we can. When we suppress our true values it can lead to low self-esteem and out-of-esteem behavior. Read about this behavior for your color group.

What To Look For When You're Out Of Esteem

There are certain symptoms you can look for when having a bad day—when you are either out or running out of esteem. You can learn to recognize these characteristics, which are generally related to your particular color grouping.

Green

Indecisiveness
Refusal to comply or cooperate
Extreme aloofness and withdrawal
Snobbish, put-down remarks, and sarcasm
Refusal to communicate; the silent treatment
Perfectionism due to severe performance anxiety
Highly critical attitudes toward yourself or others

Blue

Attention-getting misbehavior
Lying to save face
Withdrawal
Fantasy, day-dreaming, and trancing out
Crying and depression
Passive resistance
Yelling and screaming

Orange

Rudeness and defiance
Breaking the rules intentionally
Running away and dropping out
Use of stimulants
Acting out boisterously
Lying and cheating
Physical aggressiveness

True Colors

Gold

Complaining and self-pity
Anxiety and worry
Depression and fatigue
Psychosomatic problems
Malicious judgments about yourself or others
Herd mentality exhibited in blind following of leaders
Authoritarianism and phobic reactions

Exercise 6

Out-of-esteem behavior

Describe a time when you felt out-of-esteem:

_____

_____

_____

_____

_____

_____

_____

_____

True Colors

What caused you to feel this way?

What is the relationship between what triggered your out-of-esteem behavior and the things on the list of stressors?

_____

_____

_____

_____

_____

_____

Exercise 7

How to regain self-esteem

What did you do or could have done to regain your self-esteem? Reviewing your self-esteeming characteristics can be helpful.

_____

_____

_____

_____

_____

True Colors

True Colors

Self-Talk

What are you saying to yourself? Self-talk includes all the thoughts and messages we say to ourselves. It is well documented that what you say about and to yourself affects your mental, emotional and physical well being. Much of this silent, mindless chatter is negative and very destructive. Try to catch yourself when you say things like "I can't pass this class no matter what I do," or "I'm not as smart as _____."

Positive Self-Talk

You can change negative self-talk by reprogramming your mind. It is a matter of training your mind to say positive things to yourself. First you must be aware and listen to how you talk to yourself. Begin to become conscious of this behavior by recording what you say. The use of affirmations is an effective tool to change this inner dialog into positive statements about yourself. An affirmation would be to say, "I can pass this class."

Exercise 8

Negative self-talk

List some of the negative statements you have made to yourself.
Example: I'm not smart enough.

1.

2.

3.

4.

5.

6.

7.

Keep your talent in the dark and you'll never be insulted.

— Delores Ibarruri

8.

9.

10.

Change each of the negative statements into a positive one (affirmation).
Example: I am smart.

1.

2.

3.

4.

5.

6.

7.

8.

9.

10.

True Colors

Fear

Do you have everything you want in life? If not, why not? Maybe fear is blocking you-fear of failure, fear of success, fear of making the wrong decision. Fear is another barrier to block your creativity and success; it will prevent you from moving forward and giving your best.

Exercise 9

My fears

List those things you are aware of that prevent you from living your dream.
Example: Fear of public speaking

1.

2.

3.

4.

5.

A willingness to face your fear and do whatever it takes to move beyond it is the difference between a successful person and one that gives up. Which do you choose? List ways to turn the above fears around in order to achieve your goals.

Example: Take a public speaking class or hire a speech coach.

1.

2.

3.

4.

5.

True Colors

Chapter 5

Short Journal (5 minutes or less)

Write a short journal regarding a significant insight you discovered about yourself from reading this chapter.

_____

_____

_____

_____

_____

_____

_____

_____

_____

_____

_____

_____

_____

_____

_____

True Colors

True Colors

There are two kinds of talents—man-made talent and God-given talent. With man-made talent you have to work very hard. With God-given talent, you just touch it up once in a while.

— Pearl Bailey

Chapter 6

THE FOUR PATHS TO A SUCCESSFUL CAREER

Chapter 6

The Four Paths to a Successful Career

The workplace is constantly changing, and the job that is hot today may not exist by the time you have completed your education or training. Thus, it is not necessarily wise to prepare for one specific occupation.

The most important factor in career decision-making is to know what your strengths are. When you are aware of your unique gifts and talents you are in a strong position to make informed decisions about what you are interested in and what you are good at doing. Your true colors are key to unlocking these particular strengths and providing information that will give you more options to choose from.

This decision-making process can be approached by choosing either a college major or an occupation that is compatible with your interests and strengths. If you would prefer to begin with a major, think about a subject that you like—one in which you usually get your best grades—since it is important to enjoy the field of study that you choose. Or, you may want to consider a liberal arts major and the many options they offer. Though some worry they won't be able to find work if they are a liberal arts major, today's employers are more concerned about the skills you possess than your major.

It is important to know there is no direct correlation between the degree you choose and the work you will actually do. Studies show that most college graduates are successfully working in fields unrelated to their major. The following examples of three liberal arts majors—history, English and philosophy—show what some people are doing with these degrees.

What liberal arts majors are doing with a degree in:

History

In addition to working for government, politics, and education, history majors are also employed by:

- news departments of local public and commercial radio and TV stations
- newspapers
- history museums
- research and service institutions
- law firms
- firms offering preservation and restoration services
- insurance companies

For more specific career opportunities for History majors, visit the web site: www.uca.edu/history/careers.htm

English

Besides teaching and writing books, English majors are also employed by:

- newspapers
- magazines
- broadcast media-script writing
- trade, professional, or consumer publications
- advertising agencies
- libraries
- bookstores
- radio, TV, movies
- museums
- public relations firms
- corporate legal departments
- commercial bankers

For more specific career opportunities for English majors, visit the web site: www2.uncwil.edu/english/career/htm

Philosophy

In addition to teaching at colleges and universities, philosophy majors are working for:

- research/non-profit organizations
- organizations serving the arts
- religious organizations
- local, national, and international mission fields

- museums
- publishers
- political organizations
- foreign services
- national and state endowments for the Humanities
- consulting services
- public interest research groups

For more specific career opportunities for Philosophy majors, visit the web site: www.udel.edu/apa/index.html#apaonline

Adapted from information prepared by the Career Planning staff at the University of Tennessee.

Here are some more examples of liberal arts majors:

Anthropology
Art History
Biology
Chemistry
Chinese
Economics
French
Geography
German
Italian
Japanese
Mathematics
Physics
Political Science
Psychology
Sociology
Spanish
Speech

Exercise 1

Interesting liberal arts majors

Pick 2 majors and discuss how your own unique interests and strengths relate to each. Use chapter 4 to refresh your memory of your particular talents.

Major #1 _____

_____

_____

_____

_____

_____

_____

Major #2 _____

_____

_____

_____

_____

_____

_____

True Colors

Exercise 2

Appealing majors

The list below gives examples of majors that appeal to each color. Use it for more options, and circle those that appeal to you.

Blue Majors

Elementary education

Secondary education

Special education

Art therapy

Counseling

Child development

Psychology

Rehabilitation counseling

Sociology

Sign Language

Religious studies

Social work

Women's studies

Public relations

Literature

Journalism

Languages

English

Student Personnel Work

Communications

Green Majors

Classics

Law

Philosophy

Political Science

Linguistics

Architecture

Medicine

Psychiatry

Computer Science

Engineering

Biology

Veterinary Medicine

Biochemistry

Oceanography

Astronomy

Earth Sciences

Physics

Chemistry

Film making

Gold Majors

Pharmacy

Gerontology

Dentistry

Mathematics

Brokerage & Investment

Quality Control

Nursing

Accounting

Electrical Engineering
Fish & Wildlife Management
Forestry
Horticulture
Finance
Public Health
Economics
Auditing
Library Science

Banking
City Planning
Legal Assistant
Hotel-Restaurant Management
Urban Planning
Hospital Administration
Law Enforcement
Statistics

Orange Majors

Marketing
Fire Science
Auto Mechanics
Air Traffic Control
Construction Engineering
Mining Engineering
Real Estate
Radio & TV
Theater
Media
Physical Education
Music

Physical Education
Art
Design
Interior Design
Physical Therapy
Travel
Music Therapy
Recreation Administration
Cosmetology
Vocational Arts
Dance
Radio & Film Technology

Exercise 3

Universal skills

Regardless of the major you choose, some skills are of universal need in the workplace. It's not enough to only have skills in one focused area. Employers are looking for well-rounded people who can easily adapt to their work environment. Put a check mark next to the following skills you have mastered, and indicate those you need to develop with the letter "I" for **need to Improve**.

Reading _____
Writing _____
Computation _____

Oral communication _____
Creative Thinking/Problem solving _____
Computer Literacy _____
Self-esteem _____
Motivation _____
Interpersonal skills _____
Teamwork _____
Leadership _____

Short essay

How do you plan to improve in the areas marked "I"?

_____

_____

_____

_____

_____

_____

_____

_____

_____

_____

_____

True Colors

CAREER OPTIONS

The second approach to making a good career decision is to look at occupations that will utilize your natural strengths and interests. Forget about job titles and look for work that connects with what you're interested in. Your interests are the things you are curious about and those activities that give you enjoyment and satisfaction. You may think of them as the sum of your values and skills expressed in your reasons for working. This section will help you identify occupations that match your interests.

The following pages list career options that may be of interest to each of the color groups. Read all four color lists and circle those options of interest to you.

Exercise 1

Careers

Orange
Orange men and women are action oriented. They are highly resourceful and can sell a product, an idea, or a project in a way no other color type can. However, their lack of interest in administrative details and follow-through makes them the target of blame and criticism within an organization. When striking out on their own, they must have someone to follow-through if they are to be successful. When the Orange need for excitement and promotional talents are used to constructive ends, any institution is fortunate to have them as employees. However, if these energies are not channeled correctly, destructive and anti-social activities will result. Confining rules and regulations and day-to-day routines are deadly to Orange. Above all else, they seek excitement in a job.

Some examples of careers that you may find interesting are listed below. Remember, you are not limited to these options; refer to the recommended resources to generate additional options.

Circle those that are of interest to you.

Acting Coach
Actor
Advertising Sales Representative
Athletic Coach
Auto Mechanic
Bartender
Broadcast Technician
Carpenter
Cartoonist
Chef
Child Care Worker
Chiropractor
Choreographer
Clown
Comedian
Commercial Artist
Computer Operator
Computer Service Technician
Cosmetologist
Cruise Director
Dance Teacher
Dancer
Disc Jockey
Electronics Technician
Event Creation Coordinator
Fashion Illustrator
Fashion Model
Firefighter
Flight Attendant
Graphic Design Artist
Helicopter Pilot
Illustrator
Independent Video Producer
Industrial Arts Teacher
Interior Designer
Jewelry Maker
Jockey
Labor Relations Specialist
Lifeguard
Lobbyist

Magician
Marketing Specialist
Mechanical Engineer
Media Relations Executive
Mediator
Mime
Motion Picture Producer
Musician
Painter
Paramedic
Park Ranger
Party Planner
Photojournalist
Physical Education Teacher
Physical Therapist
Plumber
Police Officer
Politician
Professional Athlete
Property Manager
Public Relations Specialist
Public Speaker
Puppeteer
Race Car Driver
Radio or TV Announcer
Real Estate Agent
Restaurant Consultant
Sales Representative
Sculptor
Secret Service Agent
Set Designer
Sound Technician
Sports Nutritionist
Talent Agent
Travel Consultant
Trial Lawyer
Truck Driver
Voice-Over Artist
Waiter or Waitress
X-Ray Technician

Gold

Gold persons are realistic, matter-of-fact, and more curious about new products than they are about new ideas and theories. They are very good at following procedures and in detailing rules and regulations. They prefer work environments in which duties and authorities are well-defined, and where they can be rewarded through hard work and feel valued as responsible and dependable employees. Their interest in thoroughness, pragmatism, punctuality, and efficiency leads them to occupations in which these preferences are appreciated.

Some examples of careers that you may find interesting are listed below. Remember, you are not limited to these options; refer to the recommended resources to generate additional options.

Circle those that are of interest to you.

Accountant
Administrative Assistant
Air Traffic Controller
Archivist and Curator
Auditor
Bank Officer
Bank Teller
Bookkeeper
Budget Analyst
Business Teacher
Cashier
Claims Clerk
Closet Organizer
Collection Agent
Computer Programmer
Computer Security Specialist
Corporate Lawyer
Corrections Officer
Court Reporter
Data Entry Operator
Dental Hygienist
Dentist
Economist
Elementary School Teacher

True Colors

Financial Planner
Food Service Manager
Forester
Geneticist
Geriatric Care Manager
History Teacher
Hospital Administrator
Hotel and Restaurant Manager
Human Resource Manager
Insurance Agent
Judge
Legal Assistant
Librarian
Loan Officer
Math Teacher
Medical Billing Service
Medical Doctor
Nun
Nurse
Occupational Therapist
Paralegal/Legal Assistant
Payroll Clerk
Pharmacist
Physical Therapist
Police Officer
Public Administrator
Radiology Technician
Real Estate Agent or Broker
Receptionist
Recreational Therapist
Reservation Manager
Reunion Planner
School Administrator
School Counselor
Special Events Planner
Statistical Clerk
Statistician
Telephone Operator
Urban Planner

True Colors

Green

Greens are the most reluctant of all the color types to do things in a traditional manner. They are always on the lookout for new projects, new activities, and new procedures. This accounts for their tendency to become entrepreneurs and to work for themselves. Greens can succeed in a variety of occupations as long as the job does not involve too much hum-drum routine. They tend to lose interest once their work is no longer challenging and they may fail to follow-through, often to the discomfort of colleagues. As an employee, the Green person might work against the system just for the joy of being one-up. However, this type can contribute immensely in a work atmosphere that allows independence and expression of ingenuity.

Some examples of careers that you may find interesting are listed below. Remember, you are not limited to these options; refer to the recommended resources to generate additional options.

Circle those that are of interest to you.

Actor
Acupuncturist
Advertising Executive
Anthropologist
Architect
Art Advisor
Art Critic
Artist
Astronomer
Astrophysicist
Biomedical Engineer
Biomedical Researcher
Book Publisher
Chemist
College Professor/Researcher
Columnist
Computer Consultant
Computer Scientist
Computer systems Analyst
Consultant
Criminal Lawyer
Criminologist

Dairy Scientist
Debater
Dentist
Ecologist
Editor
Engineer
FBI Agent
Geophysicist
Ghost Writer
Grant Writer
Graphic Artist
Industrial Designer
Inventor
Journalist
Literary Agent
Lyricist
Marine Biologist
Math Teacher
Medical Doctor
Medical Researcher
Motion Picture Director
Motion Picture Producer
Movie Critic
News Writer
Newspaper Editor
Nuclear Medicine Technologist
Oceanographer
On-Line Multimedia Content Developer
Operations and Systems Researcher
Photographer
Physician's Assistant
Playwright
Podiatrist
Psychiatrist
Psychologist
Radiologist
Science Teacher
Scriptwriter
Software Programmer
Speech Pathologist

True Colors

Speech Writer
Stockbroker
Surgeon
Technical Writer
Textbook Writer
Veterinarian
Writer of Science Fiction Books

Blue

Blue persons have a remarkable latitude in career choices and they succeed in many fields. They are imaginative, enthusiastic, and can do almost anything which is of interest to them. At work, they are at ease with colleagues, and others enjoy their presence. They are highly creative in dealing with people and are outstanding at inspiring group spirit and getting people together. Blues are likely to lose interest in their job once people or projects become routine. They prefer a family-like, friendly, personalized, and warm work environment. They dislike jobs which require painstaking detail and follow-through over a period of time. They prefer people-oriented careers and job opportunities which allow creativity and variety in day-to-day operations.

Some examples of careers that you may find interesting are listed below. Remember, you are not limited to these options; refer to the recommended resources for additional options.

Circle those that are of interest to you.

Actor
Aerobics Teacher
Airline Receptionist
Art Therapist
Career Coach
Career Counselor
Community Affairs Coordinator
Drug and Alcohol Counselor
Educational Consultant
Elementary School Teacher
Employment Interviewer
English Teacher
Family Child Care Provider

Family Lawyer
Fashion Designer
Fashion Editor
Fashion Writer
Flight Attendant
Foreign Language Interpreter
Foreign Language Teacher
Foreign Language Translator
Fund-raiser
Greeting Card Writer
Gynecologist
Home Schooling Consultant
Home Tutor
Human Services Worker
Hypnotherapist
In-Home Health Care Provider
Journalist
Lawyer for Battered Women
Marketing Communication Expert
Marriage and Family Counselor
Metaphysical Teacher
Minister/Rabbi
Motivational Speaker
Music Teacher
News Reporter
Newscaster
Nun
Nutrition and Weight Loss Instructor
Pastoral Counselor
Pediatrician
Personal Coach
Poet
Psychiatric Social Worker
Psychic Reader
Psychology Teacher
Public Relations Specialist
Recreation Leader
Rehabilitation Counselor
School Counselor
Sign Language Interpreter

Singer
Skin Care Specialist
Social Science Teacher
Social Scientist
Social Worker
Speech Coach
Spiritual Counselor
Talk Show Host/Hostess
Team Building Consultant
Tour Guide
Training Specialist
Travel Agent
Wardrobe Consultant
Wedding Consultant
Writer of Children's Books
Writer of Non-Fiction Books
Writer of Romance Books

Discover more career options with the World of Work Map!

About the Map

• The map arranges job families (groups of similar jobs) into 12 regions. Together, the job families cover all U.S. jobs.

• A job family's location is based on its primary work tasks—working with DATA, IDEAS, PEOPLE, and THINGS.

• To use the map, find the job families in line with the work tasks you prefer. Then find out about the jobs in those job families.

· True Colors Codes: Orange—Courageous; Green—Conceptual; Blue—Compassionate; Gold—Conventional.

· Holland Themes: (A) Artistic; (I) Investigative; (R) Realistic; (C) Conventional; (S) Social; (E) Enterprising

· Myers-Briggs Codes: NF=Blue; NT= Green; SP=Orange; SJ= Gold

The World of Work map contains job groupings arranged by regions and work tasks. (Refer to the list on the following two pages.)

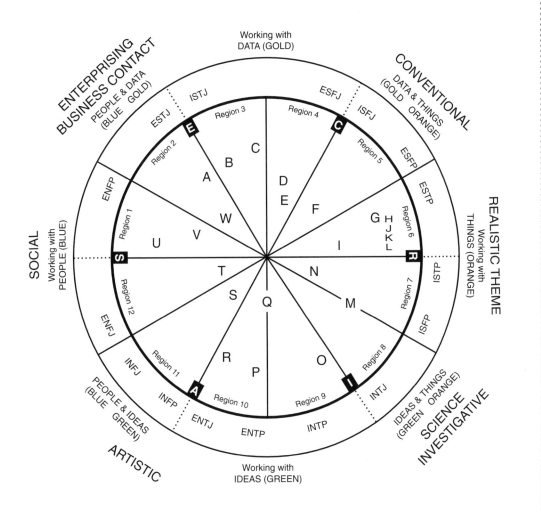

Legend

GOLD
- A. Marketing & Sales
- B. Management & Planning
- C. Records & Communication
- D. Financial Transactions
- E. Storage & Dispatching
- F. Business Machine/Computer Operation

ORANGE
- G. Vehicle Operation & Repair
- H. Construction & Maintenance
- I. Agriculture & Natural Resources
- J. Crafts & Related Services
- K. Home/Business Equipment Repair
- L. Industrial Equipment Operation & Repair

GREEN
- M. Engineering & Related Technologies
- N. Medical Specialties & Technologies
- O. Natural Sciences & Mathematics
- P. Social Sciences
- Q. Applied Arts (Visual)
- R. Creative/Performing Arts

True Colors

B
L
U
E

S. Applied Arts (Written & Spoken)

T. General Health Care

U. Education & Related Services

V. Social & Government Services

W. Personal/Customer Services

How to Find Your Career Options

Do you enjoy working with:

PEOPLE (Blue)—People you help, care for, or sell things to? See regions 12 and 1.
DATA (Gold)—Facts, numbers, files, business procedures? See regions 3 and 4.
THINGS (Orange)—Machines, tools, living things? See regions 6 and 7.
IDEAS (Green)—Using words, equations, or music? See regions 9 and 10.

This map is based on the research of The American College Testing Program — Career Planning Services (© 1984).

Exercise 2
World of Work Map

Using the World of Work Map, locate your primary job family. Look for career options below that are within your particular group, and circle those that interest you.

DATA (GOLD)
Travel agents
Insurance agents
Wholesalers
Office supply sales workers
Buyers
Purchasing agents
Small business owners

Receptionist
Office messengers
Word processor
Grocery check-out clerk
Hotel clerks
Payroll clerk
Dental assistants
Hospital attendants
Bookkeeping computer operator
Postal inspector
Plant nursery worker

PEOPLE (BLUE)

Newswriters
Reporters
Fashion Designers
Commercial Artists
Interior Decorators
Nightclub entertainers
Popular musicians
Recreation workers

THINGS (ORANGE)

Barber
Tailor
Shoemaker
Butcher
Baker
Cook
Rancher
Pet shop attendant
Sheet metal worker
Bricklayer
Bulldozer operator
Crane operator
Electrician
Printing press operator
Draftsmen
Pilot

True Colors

IDEAS (GREEN)
Medical technologist
Lab worker
Biologist
Ecologist
Statistician
Agricultural scientist
Author
Concert singer

True Colors equivalents to other personality systems that provide career information

D.O.T—Dictionary of Occupational Titles
Data	Gold
People	Blue
Things	Orange
Ideas	Green

HOLLAND THEMES—The Strong Campbell Interest Inventory
Realistic	Orange
Artistic	Blue, Green, Orange
Investigative	Green
Social	Blue
Enterprising	Orange, Green
Conventional	Gold

Keirsey—"Please Understand Me"
NF	Blue
NT	Green
SJ	Gold
SP	Orange

MBTI—Myers Briggs Type Indicator

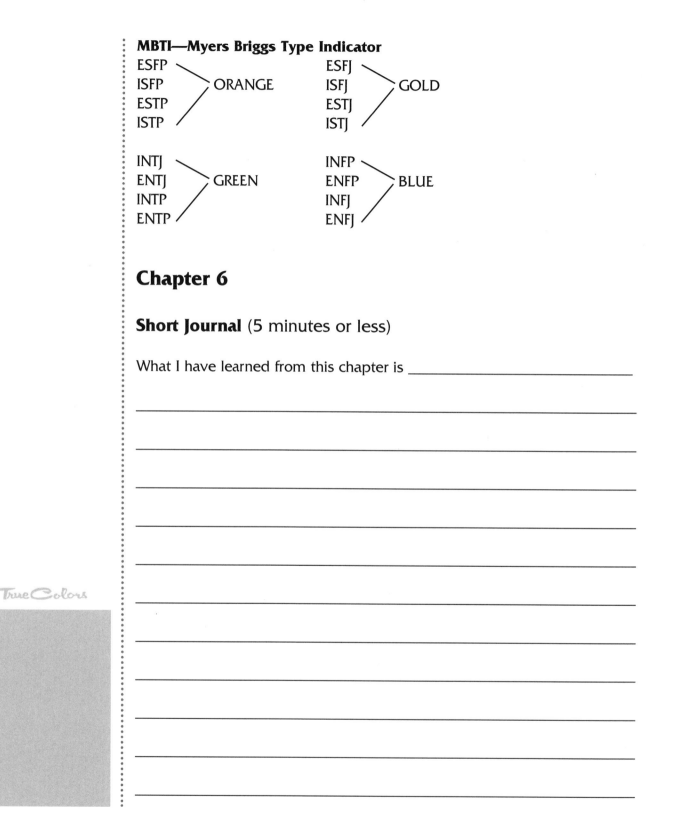

ESFP
ISFP > ORANGE
ESTP
ISTP

ESFJ
ISFJ > GOLD
ESTJ
ISTJ

INTJ
ENTJ > GREEN
INTP
ENTP

INFP
ENFP > BLUE
INFJ
ENFJ

Chapter 6

Short Journal (5 minutes or less)

What I have learned from this chapter is _____

_____

_____

_____

_____

_____

_____

_____

_____

_____

_____

True Colors

True Colors

*The only place where
success comes before work
is in a dictionary.*
— Vidal Sassoon

RESEARCH

Chapter 7

Research

How To Obtain Information About Career Options

Good decisions cannot be made without information. It is time to gather information about your top career choices in order to decide which will be most fulfilling. In addition to learning the values and skills needed for each option, you will need to know such things as duties, education/training, and salary.

You may use any of the following, as well as resources found in most libraries and college career centers, to do your research.

1. **The Dictionary of Occupational Titles (DOT)** lists over 35,000 job titles and more than 20,000 different occupations. A job description is given with skills required for each occupation.

2. **The Occupational Outlook Handbook (OOH)** includes information on job descriptions, places of employment, training, educational requirements, and salary ranges. The salary information is national and, therefore, the estimates will be low for the greater Los Angeles area.

3. **The ONET-Occupational Information Network** is a computer database designed to replace the DOT and OOH.

4. **The Guide for Occupational Exploration (GOE)** is based on worker trait group interests that relate to possible occupations.

True Colors

You may want to check out these career assessment web sites:

1. www.truecolorscareer.com

This site offers information about the book **Follow Your True Colors to the Work You Love.**

2. www.truecolors.org

This web site gives an assessment as well as other information about the True Colors program.

3. www.keirsey.com

This site offers The Keirsey Character Sorter and The Keirsey Temperament Sorter based on the Myers-Briggs personality types.

4. www2.ncsu.edu/unity/lockers/users/l/lkj

The Career Key offers a free public service to help people make sound career decisions (based on Holland's theory).

5. www.self-directed-search.com

A career assessment based on the Self-Directed Search ($7.95 as of July 1999).

Career centers usually will have one of these resourceful systems.

1. **Discover** is a complete computer-based career information and planning system. You may go directly to the "information only" file for occupational information.

2. **Eureka** is a California career information system that delivers occupational and educational information on 390 occupations, 140 programs of study and training, 221 post-secondary schools in California, and more than 1,700 colleges and universities in the United States.

Exercise 1

Worksheets

Use the following career research worksheets to answer questions about each of your 5 or more options.

CAREER RESEARCH WORKSHEET

Position title: _____

Description of duties and responsibilities: _____

_____

_____

_____

Where to look for this type of career: _____

_____

_____

Education, training, or experience required: _____

_____

_____

_____

True Colors

Beneficial personal qualities: _____

_____

_____

Expected earnings: _____

Immediate outlook for this career (1-5 years): _____

_____

_____

_____

Long-term outlook (5-10 years): _____

_____

_____

_____

True Colors

Sources and references: _____

_____

_____

_____

_____

CAREER RESEARCH WORKSHEET

Position title: _____

Description of duties and responsibilities: _____

_____

_____

_____

Where to look for this type of career: _____

_____

_____

Education, training, or experience required: _____

_____

_____

_____

Beneficial personal qualities: _____

_____

_____

True Colors

Expected earnings: _____

Immediate outlook for this career (1-5 years): _____

_____

_____

_____

_____

Long-term outlook (5-10 years): _____

_____

_____

_____

_____

Sources and references: _____

_____

_____

_____

_____

True Colors

CAREER RESEARCH WORKSHEET

Position title: _____

Description of duties and responsibilities: _____

_____

_____

_____

Where to look for this type of career: _____

_____

_____

Education, training, or experience required: _____

_____

_____

_____

Beneficial personal qualities: _____

_____

_____

True Colors

Expected earnings: _____

Immediate outlook for this career (1-5 years): _____

_____

_____

_____

_____

Long-term outlook (5-10 years): _____

_____

_____

_____

_____

Sources and references: _____

_____

_____

_____

_____

_____

TrueColors

CAREER RESEARCH WORKSHEET

Position title: _____

Description of duties and responsibilities: _____

_____

_____

_____

Where to look for this type of career: _____

_____

_____

Education, training, or experience required: _____

_____

_____

_____

Beneficial personal qualities: _____

_____

_____

True Colors

Expected earnings: _____

Immediate outlook for this career (1-5 years): _____

_____

_____

_____

_____

Long-term outlook (5-10 years): _____

_____

_____

_____

_____

Sources and references: _____

_____

_____

_____

_____

True Colors

CAREER RESEARCH WORKSHEET

Position title: _____

Description of duties and responsibilities: _____

_____

_____

_____

Where to look for this type of career: _____

_____

_____

Education, training, or experience required: _____

_____

_____

_____

Beneficial personal qualities: _____

_____

_____

True Colors

Expected earnings: _____

Immediate outlook for this career (1-5 years): _____

_____

_____

_____

_____

Long-term outlook (5-10 years): _____

_____

_____

_____

_____

Sources and references: _____

_____

_____

_____

_____

True Colors

CAREER RESEARCH WORKSHEET

Position title: _____

Description of duties and responsibilities: _____

_____

_____

_____

Where to look for this type of career: _____

_____

_____

Education, training, or experience required: _____

_____

_____

_____

Beneficial personal qualities: _____

_____

_____

Expected earnings: _____

Immediate outlook for this career (1-5 years): _____

_____

_____

_____

_____

Long-term outlook (5-10 years): _____

_____

_____

_____

_____

Sources and references: _____

_____

_____

_____

_____

True Colors

CAREER RESEARCH WORKSHEET

Position title: _____

Description of duties and responsibilities: _____

_____

_____

_____

Where to look for this type of career: _____

_____

_____

Education, training, or experience required: _____

_____

_____

_____

Beneficial personal qualities: _____

_____

_____

True Colors

Expected earnings: _____

Immediate outlook for this career (1-5 years): _____

_____

_____

_____

_____

Long-term outlook (5-10 years): _____

_____

_____

_____

_____

Sources and references: _____

_____

_____

_____

_____

True Colors

TYING IT ALL TOGETHER

The information provided should have given some options to help make a decision about the direction you want to take in your career. To experience satisfaction in your work it is important to be who you are by expressing your true values, and do what you love by using your best skills. Your career decision could eventually lead to your life's work—your ultimate career. The exercise below will help you evaluate your choices and clarify their soundness.

Exercise 2

Clarifying your values, skills, and occupations

Your values clarify how you need to express yourself in your work. List 5 or more of your most important values from chapter 4.

1. _____

2. _____

3. _____

4. _____

5. _____

6. _____

7. _____

When you are able to use your best skills, you enjoy what you do. List 5 or more of your most enjoyable skills from chapter 4.

1. _____

2. _____

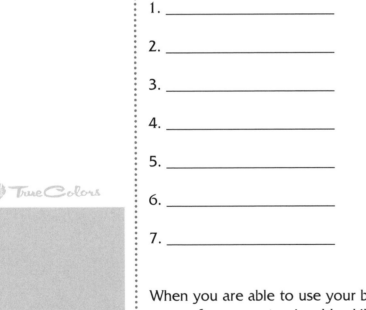

True Colors

3. _____

4. _____

5. _____

6. _____

7. _____

List 5 of the top career choices from your completed research sheets.

1. _____

2. _____

3. _____

4. _____

5. _____

6. _____

7. _____

Exercise 3

Career Summary

Complete one of the following sheets for each of your 5 career choices. If you cannot provide the requested information, maybe you need to consider other options more related to your values and skills.

Career #1 _____

List the values you will express in this work.

_____

_____

_____

_____

_____

_____

Explain how you will express each value.

_____

_____

_____

_____

_____

_____

_____

_____

True Colors

List the skills you will use in this work.

_____

_____

_____

_____

_____

Explain how you will use each skill.

_____

_____

_____

_____

_____

_____

_____

_____

True Colors

Career #2 _____

List the values you will express in this work.

_____

_____

_____

_____

_____

_____

Explain how you will express each value.

_____

_____

_____

_____

_____

_____

_____

True Colors

List the skills you will use in this work.

_____

_____

_____

_____

_____

_____

Explain how you will use each skill.

_____

_____

_____

_____

_____

_____

_____

_____

True Colors

Career #3 _____

List the values you will express in this work.

_____

_____

_____

_____

_____

_____

_____

Explain how you will express each value.

_____

_____

_____

_____

_____

_____

_____

_____

_____

True Colors

List the skills you will use in this work.

_____

_____

_____

_____

_____

_____

Explain how you will use each skill.

_____

_____

_____

_____

_____

_____

_____

_____

_____

True Colors

Career #4 _____

List the values you will express in this work.

_____

_____

_____

_____

_____

_____

Explain how you will express each value.

_____

_____

_____

_____

_____

_____

_____

_____

_____

True Colors

List the skills you will use in this work.

_____

_____

_____

_____

_____

_____

Explain how you will use each skill.

_____

_____

_____

_____

_____

_____

_____

_____

True Colors

Career #5 _____

List the values you will express in this work.

_____

_____

_____

_____

_____

_____

Explain how you will express each value.

_____

_____

_____

_____

_____

_____

_____

_____

True Colors

List the skills you will use in this work.

_____

_____

_____

_____

_____

_____

Explain how you will use each skill.

_____

_____

_____

_____

_____

_____

_____

_____

_____

True Colors

Chapter 7

Short Journal (5 minutes or less)

What I have learned about myself in this chapter is _____

_____

_____

_____

_____

_____

_____

_____

_____

_____

_____

_____

_____

_____

_____

_____

_____

True Colors

True Colors

Knowledge is of two kinds.
We know a subject ourselves,
or we know where we can
find information upon it.
— Samuel Johnson

Chapter
8

INFORMATIONAL
INTERVIEWING

Chapter 8

Informational Interviewing

What is an informational interview?

An informational interview is a great way to gather information from an expert in a particular field. It is the simple method of talking with someone about their area of work, and asking questions about how they got started and what it's like to do the work they do. All it requires is for you to ask questions—let the other person do most of the talking.

How do I interview someone for information?

You are now ready to choose one of the occupations you have researched and talk to someone who works in that field about what the job is really like on a day-to-day basis. This is also called "networking." Be sure your contacts understand that the purpose of these interviews is not to find a job, but to gather personal information regarding the occupation or profession. Most people love to talk about their work.

Use the telephone book, career files and directories, instructors, and friends or relatives to assist you in locating local organizations in the fields of your interest. Call for an appointment with the appropriate person or ask the personnel department to suggest someone.

As you go through this exercise, remember that you are seeking a career that is esteeming to you; be alert for those characteristics of the work environment and personnel that will identify specific color groupings. It is important to your future that your values and your natural skills and talents be compatible with your work.

Ask to interview the person at their place of employment. This will provide an opportunity for you to observe the working environment. And remember the following:

• Make a good impression—you may want to return to request employment.
• Be on time and dress appropriately.
• If you must cancel or reschedule the appointment, call to let them know.

True Colors

• Take notes during the interview and ask questions.
• Ask for a business card.
• Send a thank-you note for the person's time and assistance.

Exercise 1

Interview questions

Answer the following questions about each interview.

1. Date and time of interview? _____

2. Name and job title of person interviewed? _____

3. Description of a typical workday? _____

_____

_____

_____

_____

4. Qualifications for job? _____

_____

5. How did this person break into this field? _____

_____

_____

True Colors

6. What is the job market like? _____

_____

_____

_____

7. What are starting salaries? _____

8. What are advancement opportunities? _____

_____

_____

_____

9. What did you think of the working environment? _____

_____

_____

_____

10. In light of this interview, are you encouraged or discouraged about this occupation as a possible career?

_____

_____

_____

_____

True Colors

Exercise 2

Personality characteristics of person interviewed

1. Can you identify the color group of the person you interviewed? _____

2. Is your color the same or different? _____

3. Describe the communication between the two of you with reference to your color groups.

_____

_____

_____

_____

_____

4. How did this impact your decision about the career? _____

_____

_____

_____

_____

REMEMBER: The information you are receiving is coming through their color filter. You will ultimately have to make a decision that is based on your own personality values, skills, and interests.

True Colors

Chapter 8

Short Journal (5 minutes or less)

What did you learn from this interview?

_____

_____

_____

_____

_____

_____

_____

_____

_____

_____

_____

_____

_____

_____

_____

_____

True Colors

True Colors

*I have found the best way
to give advice to your
children is to find out
what they want and
then advise them to do it.*

— Harry S. Truman

Chapter

9

FAMILY INFLUENCE ON CAREER DECISIONS

CHAPTER 9

Family Influence on Career Decisions

Take out your color-coded Character Cards and rank order them as you did before, but this time rank them for each of your parents. You may ask your parents to rank their own cards. List their primary colors below:

Father: _____

Mother: _____

Myself: _____

Parents usually set the tone for the family. When a person is not understood by the parents, the cause may be the clash of color codes and, therefore, a mixture of values. You may be able to relate to this information even if you left home several years ago, and see how your parent's influence, positive or negative, caused you to go in the career direction you have chosen.

On pages that follow, color combinations illustrate probable family reactions when the same and different parent/child color combinations are present. But first read about the parenting style of each personality (color).

GREEN parents will focus on their kids intellectual ability. This will start when the baby is in the crib by buying stimulating toys for them. Instead of saying "goo-goo ga-ga" they will speak in adult language to these infants. They will also begin to read to their babies very early. As soon as their kids can talk they will teach them to speak clearly and in complete sentences. Their children will usually have a large vocabulary very early. Because they don't believe in fostering dependency, they will insist on their kids using their own minds to problem solve and make decisions. They may insist that their child look up an answer in the encyclopedia instead of asking the parents. Children are treated like little adults. Reading and learning are very important to these parents so they will encourage their kids to do the same. Family outings will likely include places like the library and the museum.

BLUE parents are not usually big on discipline. They tend to treat their children in a more democratic way that takes everyone's needs into consideration. Much focus is placed on their kids' emotional well being. It is important to them that their children are happy and feel good about themselves. They like to hug and kiss their kids a lot. They also value self-esteem so highly that they will stress positive things about their kids and sometimes overlook the negative.

Disharmony is so upsetting to them that they strive to keep peace among family members. These parents like to talk to their kids and have them openly express their feelings. If something is bothering the child, a Blue parent will be the first to know. Maintaining a close relationship with their kids is most important to these parents. Often you will see Blue mothers and daughters shopping and doing things together like best girl friends. They encourage their kids to have friends so it is not unusual for them to entertain other kids in their home.

Orange parents probably play this role in the least traditional manner. They are more permissive with their kids and give them more freedom to make decisions. They are also more playful with their kids and sometimes treat them like peers. Other times they will take back their authority role, but they punish less often and with less severity than Gold parents. There tends to be more flexibility in the home in general. Kids may not always go to bed at the same time at night depending on what else is going on in the home, and meals may be served when everyone feels like eating rather than at established times. They like to go out to eat, a decision, like many others, that is often based on how they feel at the moment.

GOLD parents play their role in the most traditional manner. They establish themselves as the authority figures in the family and demand that children respect them as such. The parents determine the rules that govern the family, and the children are taught to obey these rules or they will be punished. These parents are usually very strict with their kids. Discipline plays a major part in their parenting style and this discipline does not stop at home. They also demand that their children be good citizens who obey the law and other authority figures outside of the home, such as teachers and ministers.

Parental Color Influences on the Orange Student

Orange Parents
This is a great match! These two share the same values, interests, and energy. Being of the same color group, they are compatible and easily understand

each other. Parent and child of the Orange group will tend to be very active, adventurous, and will seek excitement. Both will compete, enjoy hands-on activities, and be physical and spontaneous. They may encounter some difficulty arising from competing against each other, or they may create a game of "one-upping" the other.

Gold Parents

This can be a difficult match. It is the classic family clash. These two have very different values and often disagree sharply. The Orange child is a risk-taker desiring action, spontaneity, and adventure. The Gold parent holds traditional values and morals with a definite sense of right and wrong. Treasuring stability, responsibility, and predictability, the Gold parent may have difficulty with the Orange child's impulsiveness, fun-loving spirit, immediate gratification attitude, and drive. The child may also rebel against the rules imposed and their Gold parent's planned, serious approach to life.

Green Parents

The Green parent and the Orange child share values of getting to the point and in being direct. They are also similar in the drive to compete and to be competent. Difficulties arise when the Green parent's futuristic, abstract thinking conflicts with the Orange child's drive for "here and now" action. The controlling nature of the Green parent (who has high expectations for perfection and excellence) may be met with rebellion from the Orange child. A big contrast exists with the Orange child who seeks external stimulation and entertainment and the Green parent strives to instill internal motivation and quests.

Blue Parents

This combination tends to work, although often at the expense of the Orange child who is learning responsibility. Conflicts can arise due to the Blue parent's talent of empathizing and appreciating uniqueness. At times, the Orange child receives too much flexibility in being himself/herself and does not receive necessary discipline; the child may rebel against the parent's need to communicate and to relate. Orange children are often appreciated and encouraged to be creative and seek possibilities. But the push for honesty and authenticity by the Blue parent may be considered intrusive to the Orange independence. The Blue parent may be seen by the Orange child as a soft-touch, too mellow, and easily manipulated—an art of the Orange child.

True Colors

Parental Color Influences on the Gold Student

Orange Parents

The biggest frustration in this combination is the Orange parent's lifestyle of few rules and little structure compared to the Gold child who wants tradition, plans, predictability, and who carries a sense of right and wrong. The playful attitude and spontaneous ventures of the parent is sometimes fun for the child, yet can be embarrassing, as well. Gold children share a need for usefulness of ideas or objects. A cluttered home that the Orange parent allows may be unsightly to the Gold child. The Gold child will tend to worry over the Orange parent's impulsiveness to conquer the unknown.

Gold Parents

This match is brilliant—a golden combination that satisfies and supports both the parents and the child. Both enjoy the clearly defined expectations and the rules established in the household. Things are neat, orderly, and run on a schedule. The consistency and stability of the home is comforting to both parents and child. They mutually support and adhere to tradition and to the laws of home and society. There is a clear sense of the parent being in charge. A great deal of hard work occurs at home and both parents and children excel in work and in school.

Green Parents

The Gold child may have difficulty with the futuristic, abstract thinking of the Green parent. The child wants more detailed, organized, practical guidance. The Green parent's high expectations for competency and perfection will motivate the Gold child to do well, yet may be perceived as too demanding after a reasonable standard has been met.

Blue Parents

This combination shares values of belonging and helping others. Areas of potential difficulty involve the Blue parent's idealistic, searching imagination, which conflicts with the Gold child's need for practical, outlined structure. The Blue parent may be seen as "wishy-washy" and not providing enough "backbone" for family. Often, the Blue parent's searching involves non-traditional activities viewed as ridiculous to the Gold student.

True Colors

Parental Color Influences on the Green Student

Orange Parents

These two share values of freedom to explore what interests them. They tend to allow room for the other to seek stimulating experiences. The Green child thrives on ideas and invention, while the Orange parent quests for adventure on a physical level. The parent may joke about the child being "too stuffy," and the child may joke that the parent is "too wild" or "off the wall." However, they award each other mutual respect, even though the Orange parent may not measure up to the Green child's high expectations of perfectionism.

Gold Parents

There are often clashes in this combination. The Gold parent wants to instill in the child values of planning and preparing for a secure future of family, savings, and a dependable, respectable job. The Green child tends to value the quest for abstract, futuristic ideas for the sake of invention and the mental challenge. They both tend to have a serious approach to life and avoid physical risks. The Green child is very independent and the Gold parent wants to bring him/her into the family unit more than the child desires.

Green Parents

Because parent and child share the same values, this is a compatible combination. The Green parent and child stimulate and challenge one another's logic, inventions, and wisdom. Both drive for competency and perfection, and feed off each other's projects. They respect each other's need for independence and understand the distance in relationships. Both are powerful people, and there may be some clashes and competition with competency. The child may feel the need to be as good as or better than the parent, and the parent's need to maintain status and control will conflict.

Blue Parents

The Green child often feels smothered by the Blue parent. The parent's need for communication, for family cohesion, and for emotional connections is uncomfortable and often viewed as silly by the Green child. The Blue parent's feelings of focus and fostering dependency on family is the exact opposite of the Green child's quest for knowledge and independence.

True Colors

Parental Color Influences on the Blue Student

Orange Parents
The Blue child has an understanding of the parent's need for adventure and impulsive actions. The child enjoys the parent's fun-loving sense of humor, but is easily hurt by the parent's to-the-point directness. Parent and child share the quest for possibilities, yet the parent is the greater risk-taker of the two. The Blue child is not competitive like the parent, but rather seeks cohesion, harmony, and a "working together" relationship. The Blue child can seem too needy to the on-the-go Orange parent. The Blue child may feel neglected and a lack of being nurtured.

Gold Parents
The Blue child complies with the Gold parent's rules and structure at home, yet may behave differently with friends in order to fit in. Parent and child share the need to belong and the dependency on family. They separate as the Blue child grows older and relies more on friends. The Blue child strives for harmony and may not be direct with the truth with the Gold parent who expects adherence to right and wrong, according to the rules of the family. The Blue child's idealism and the realism of the Gold parent can at times clash.

Green Parents
This combination often leaves the Blue child starved for attention due to the Green parent's preoccupation with ideas and abstractions. The parent's need for independence and distance from frequent emotional connections or demonstrations overshadows the Blue Child's striving for affection, relating, and communicating. The child's value of sensitivity and empathy of feelings is in opposition to the parent's value of logic and knowledge. The Blue child may feel the Green parent is too harsh and demanding in expecting competency and perfection. The child may strive to meet these expectations to please and may never feel quite good enough.

Blue Parents
This is a satisfying combination for both parent and child. The compatibility of their values meets needs for relationships, communication, sensitivity, and understanding. This combination can also result in an extremely dependent parent/child relationship to the detriment of both. The child may put so much energy into taking care of and pleasing the parent that he/she becomes stunted in terms of mental development.

Exercise 1

Relationship with your mother

Which combination describes your relationship with your mother?

_____

_____

What insights have you gained from the description?

_____

_____

_____

_____

_____

Compare your values with those of your mother. Discuss how they are compatible or how they clash.

_____

_____

_____

_____

_____

_____

How does your mother feel about your career choices?

_____

_____

_____

_____

_____

_____

What impact has this had on you?

_____

_____

_____

_____

_____

_____

_____

True Colors

Exercise 2

Relationship with your father

Which combination describes your relationship with your father?

_____

_____

What insights have you gained from the description?

_____

_____

_____

_____

_____

Compare your values with those of your father. Discuss how they are compatible or how they clash.

_____

_____

_____

_____

_____

_____

True Colors

How does you father feel about your career choices?

_____

_____

_____

_____

_____

_____

What impact has this had on you?

_____

_____

_____

_____

_____

_____

When you understand that people see the world through their own filters, you will see why your parents may view the world differently than you. Therefore, you will also see why the career choices they might want for you may be different from the choices you make for yourself.

Chapter 9

Short Journal (5 minutes or less)

What I have learned about myself in this chapter is _____

_____

_____

_____

_____

_____

_____

_____

_____

_____

_____

_____

_____

_____

_____

_____

True Colors

A teacher affects eternity;
he can never tell where
his influence stops.
— Henry Brooks Adams

Chapter

10

TEACHER'S
INFLUENCE

Chapter 10

Teacher's Influence

Teaching Styles

Teaching styles differ depending on the teacher's color or personality. Personal values dictate what motivates a person's behavior and therefore indicates what your teachers will focus their attention on in the classroom. The lists below show the values of each color teacher.

The Orange Teacher Values:
Spontaneity
Creativity
The unusual and out-of-the-ordinary
Hands-on activities
Concrete materials
Immediate results
Short-term goals
Energy, vitality, movement
Physical activity
Cleverness
Attention
Skills

The Gold Teacher Values:
Student achievement and performance
Proper student behavior
Lack of classroom disruptions
Student punctuality
Classroom rules established and obeyed
Organization and structure
Tradition (the tried and true)
Lecture method of delivering instruction
Subject-oriented classroom activities
Exactness
Hard work
Long-term goals

The Green Teacher Values:
Freedom
Independent thought
Mental activity
Individuality
Ingenuity
Self-control
Competence
Subject- or knowledge-oriented classroom activities
Independent study and projects
Problem-solving approach to instruction
Inquiry and discovery methods of instruction
Future outcomes

The Blue Teacher Values:
Being able to relate to students on a personal level
Giving help to students (academic and social)
A "good feeling tone" in his/her classroom
The esteem of all those in his/her class
Harmony
Understanding
People-oriented concepts and activities
Influencing others for their "good"
Cooperative learning
Imagination and creativity
Success for everyone

Personal Motivation Determines Learning Styles . . . and Which Teachers are Compatible

The purpose of this chapter is to reveal your ideal teacher, discuss your ideal learning environment, and help you understand what motivates you to learn. Because we don't all learn the same way, it is important to know what motivates you. This knowledge will help you understand why you learn from some teachers and not from others.

Respond to the following according to your first color.

ORANGE STUDENTS

Learning Motivators
- Perform well in competition, especially when there is a lot of action
- Love games and "hands-on" activities
- Love fun and excitement
- Have difficulty with routine or structured presentations
- Receive a kick out of putting what they have learned to immediate use
- Perform best when they can apply skills learned in school to the world
- in which they live
- Learn by doing

Atmosphere in which Orange Students Learn Best
- Spontaneous
- Animated, active
- Humorous
- Interactive
- Minimal lectures
- Friendly

Exercise 1

Positive learning experience

Give an example of a positive learning experience that you have had.

_____

_____

_____

_____

_____

_____

_____

_____

_____

_____

_____

_____

What is the relationship between this experience and what motivates you to learn?

_____

_____

_____

_____

_____

_____

_____

True Colors

Looking at Teachers from the Orange Perspective

Orange Teacher: A good match with the Orange student. The student is likely to maintain the greatest rapport with an Orange teacher. The student appreciates the atmosphere of freedom and spontaneity in this teacher's classroom and responds favorably to the "hands-on" approach to learning. Both teacher and student enjoy games and competition and are tireless in their efforts to complete any job at hand.

Exercise 2

Experience with an Orange teacher

Describe an experience that you had with this type of teacher.

_____

_____

_____

_____

_____

_____

_____

_____

_____

_____

_____

True Colors

Looking at Teachers from the Orange Perspective

Gold Teacher: The Gold teacher's demands for order, organization, and appropriate behavior in the classroom do not conform well with the Orange student's need for spontaneity, fun, and quick action. The Gold teacher emphasizes rules and facts, as well as neatness and structure. The Orange student may react with various degrees of rebellion and hostility when confronted with a Gold classroom atmosphere.

Exercise 3

Experience with a Gold teacher

Describe an experience you had with this type of teacher.

_____

_____

_____

_____

_____

_____

_____

_____

_____

_____

True Colors

Looking at Teachers from the Orange Perspective

Green Teacher: The Green teacher is often capable of creating an atmosphere of independence, freedom of thought, and action in his classroom. This climate allows the Orange student to express his needs.

Exercise 4

Experience with a Green teacher

Describe an experience that you had with this type of teacher.

_____

_____

_____

_____

_____

_____

_____

_____

_____

_____

_____

True Colors

Looking at Teachers from the Orange Perspective

Blue Teacher: The Blue teacher can have some empathy for the Orange student's needs, and this teacher's good sense of humor is protection from reacting too harshly to the Orange student's demands for fun and entertainment. The Orange student may require more "hands-on" activities, games, and competition than are normally scheduled in the lesson plans of the Blue teacher.

Exercise 5

Experience with a Blue teacher

Describe an experience that you had with this type of teacher.

_____

_____

_____

_____

_____

_____

_____

_____

_____

_____

True Colors

GOLD STUDENTS

Learning Motivators

· Do their best when the course content is structured and clearly defined
· Want to know when they are on the right track
· Are greatly helped by rules and directions
· Thrive on routine and orderliness

Atmosphere in which Gold Students Learn Best

· Structured
· Tasks clearly stated
· Organized
· Clear expectations

Exercise 1

Positive learning experiences

Give an example of a positive learning experience that you have had.

_____

_____

_____

_____

What is the relationship between this experience and what motivates you to learn?

_____

_____

_____

_____

Looking at Teachers from the Gold Perspective

Orange Teacher: This combination can be somewhat problematic. The Gold student prefers organized, structured, and predictable routines, while the Orange teacher tends to prefer an atmosphere of spontaneity and excitement. The Gold student may often complain that tasks are never completed and that he does not learn much of anything in the Orange teacher's classroom. The Gold student strives for perfection and enjoys being validated for neat and accurate work.

Exercise 2

Experience with an Orange teacher

Describe an experience that you had with this type of teacher.

_____

_____

_____

_____

_____

_____

_____

_____

_____

Looking at Teachers from the Gold Perspective

Gold Teacher: This is a suitable match. The Gold student is likely to maintain the greatest rapport and cooperation with the Gold teacher. The student appreciates the structure, organization, and rules that the Gold teacher emphasizes. The Gold student responds well to this teacher's style of presenting material which is based on logical procedures and clearly defined factual information.

Exercise 3

Experience with a Gold teacher

Describe an experience that you had with this type of teacher.

_____

_____

_____

_____

_____

_____

_____

_____

_____

_____

_____

True Colors

Looking at Teachers from the Gold Perspective

Green Teacher: The Green teacher may not always meet the needs of the Gold student for clear and concise rules and regulations. The independent thinking, originality, and mental creativity so valued by this Green teacher will not be highly appreciated by the Gold student. The Gold student may experience anxiety and difficulty related to grasping conceptual matter if it is not explained and demonstrated in concrete ways.

Exercise 4

Experience with a Green teacher

Describe an experience that you had with this type of teacher.

_____

_____

_____

_____

_____

_____

_____

_____

_____

True Colors

Looking at Teachers from the Gold Perspective

Blue Teacher: The Gold student responds well to the Blue teacher's classroom atmosphere if a regular and predictable schedule is maintained. The Gold student requires rules and facts, as well as organized, accurate, and logical procedures. The Blue teacher and the Gold student may differ in expression of response to very deep emotions. Although the Gold student follows rules and accomplishes well-structures work, the creativity valued by the Blue teacher may rarely be exhibited.

Exercise 5

Experience with a Blue teacher

Describe an experience that you had with this type of teacher.

_____

_____

_____

_____

_____

_____

_____

_____

_____

_____

_____

GREEN STUDENTS

Learning Motivators

· Perform best when exposed to the driving force or overall theory behind a subject
· Prefer to work independently
· Aroused by new ideas and concepts, and enjoy interpreting them before adding them to their bank of knowledge
· Need to be challenged
· Like to be recognized and appreciated for their competence in a subject

Atmosphere in which Green Students Learn Best

· Academically demanding
· Encouragement to learn more
· Energetic programs

Exercise 1

Positive learning experiences

Give an example of a positive learning experience that you have had.

_____

_____

_____

_____

What is the relationship between this experience and what motivates you to learn?

_____

_____

_____

_____

True Colors

Looking at Teachers from the Green Perspective

Orange Teacher: The Green student responds well to the classroom atmosphere of the Orange teacher if attracted to the subject matter, and if allowed to express and discuss personal ideas. The Green student is creative and enjoys discovering new ways of solving problems. Unlike the Orange teacher, the Green student values ideas and concepts above immediate action and wants to inquire about the principles behind each task.

Exercise 2

Experience with an Orange teacher

Describe an experience that you had with this type of teacher.

_____

_____

_____

_____

_____

_____

_____

_____

_____

_____

True Colors

Looking at Teachers from the Green Perspective

Gold Teacher: This combination works only if the Green student is sufficiently interested in the subject matter and given some freedom to explore ideas and concepts beyond the requirements of the class. Unlike the Gold teacher, the Green student can be oblivious to rules and regulations. It will be difficult to gain the Green student's cooperation without a perception that rules are logical and necessary.

Exercise 3

Experience with a Gold teacher

Describe an experience that you had with this type of teacher.

_____

_____

_____

_____

_____

_____

_____

_____

_____

_____

True Colors

Looking at Teachers from the Green Perspective

Green Teacher: The Green student will likely maintain the greatest rapport and cooperation with Green teachers. The student appreciates the stimulating and creative environment provided by the Green teacher and enjoys discussing ideas, investigating relationships between principles, and discovering new ways of solving problems—especially in conjunction with the Green teacher.

Exercise 4

Experience with a Green teacher

Describe an experience that you had with this type of teacher.

_____

_____

_____

_____

_____

_____

_____

_____

_____

_____

True Colors

Looking at Teachers from the Green Perspective

Blue Teacher: The Green student responds well to the classroom atmosphere of the Blue teacher, as long as the student's interest in the subject matter and curiosity is continually reinforced. Unlike the Blue teacher, the Green student is less concerned with the feelings of others and will tend to express opinions regardless of how they may affect the feelings of others.

Exercise 5

Experience with a Blue teacher

Describe an experience that you had with this type of teacher.

_____

_____

_____

_____

_____

_____

_____

_____

True Colors

BLUE STUDENTS

Learning Motivators

- Feel best in an open, interactive atmosphere
- Like to feel that their teachers really care about them, and that they give the class a personal touch
- Appreciate supportive attention and feedback
- Thrive in a "humanistic," people-oriented environment
- "Turn-off" when conflicts arise, and flourish in an atmosphere of cooperation
- Important that teachers value and respect their feelings

Atmosphere in which Blue Students Learn Best

- Warm
- Relaxed
- Creative
- Flexible
- Personal
- Caring, happy
- Discussion-oriented
- Freedom to experiment

Exercise 1

Positive learning experiences

Give an example of a positive learning experience that you have had.

_____

_____

_____

_____

_____

_____

What is the relationship between this experience and what motivates you to learn?

_____

_____

_____

_____

Looking at Teachers from the Blue Perspective

Orange Teacher: This combination can work well if the Orange teacher allows the Blue student to be creative and show personal concern. The Blue student appreciates the good sense of humor of the Orange teacher. The student may have difficulty making quick decisions and could become bogged down before completing a task. Although the Blue student values communication and social interaction, the Orange teacher's direct mode of criticism and comments may not be appreciated.

Exercise 2

Experience with an Orange teacher

Describe an experience that you had with this type of teacher.

_____

_____

_____

_____

_____

True Colors

_____

_____

_____

_____

_____

_____

_____

Looking at Teachers from the Blue Perspective

Gold Teacher: The Blue student adheres to the rules of the Gold teacher as long as they seem fair and there is personal consideration and compassion given to the student. The Blue student will cooperate, particularly if it is felt the Gold teacher likes and cares for the individuality of the student. Unlike the Gold teacher, the Blue student tends to be emotional and allow feelings to interfere with academic work. This student's need to socialize may also be viewed as highly disruptive by the Gold teacher.

Exercise 3

Experience with a Gold teacher

Describe an experience that you had with this type of teacher.

_____

_____

_____

_____

_____

True Colors

_____

_____

_____

_____

_____

_____

Looking at Teachers from the Blue Perspective

Green Teacher: The Blue student responds well to the classroom atmosphere of the Green teacher, as long as it is personally relevant and stimulating to a creative imagination. The Blue student is motivated to perform in an effort to please the teacher, rather than to demonstrate intellectual mastery of a concept. Unlike the Green teacher, this student tends to value feelings and interpersonal communication above ideas and concepts. Some potential for friction exists due to this difference in values.

Exercise 4

Experience with a Green teacher

Describe an experience that you had with this type of teacher.

_____

_____

_____

_____

_____

_____

_____

_____

_____

_____

_____

_____

Looking at Teachers from the Blue Perspective

Blue Teacher: The Blue student will likely maintain the greatest rapport and cooperation with the Blue teacher. The Blue student appreciates the fairness, sensitivity, and personal concern expressed by the Blue teacher. The atmosphere of imaginative creativity and social interaction provided by the Blue teacher is highly appealing to the Blue student.

Exercise 5

Experience with a Blue teacher

Describe an experience that you had with this type of teacher.

_____

_____

_____

_____

_____

_____

_____

_____

_____

_____

_____

_____

_____

Exercise 6

Determining True Colors of Teachers

List your current instructors and their True Colors. If you cannot determine their color groups, ask them to rank the cards themselves.

1. _____

2. _____

3. _____

4. _____

5. _____

Now, discuss your learning experiences with each instructor.

1. _____

_____

_____

_____

2. _____

_____

_____

_____

3. _____

_____

_____

_____

True Colors

4. _____

_____

_____

_____

5. _____

_____

_____

_____

You may not always have your ideal teacher for every class. But by understanding what motivates you to learn and the atmosphere in which you learn best, you will be able to take more responsibility for your own experience.

Exercise 7

Multiple Intelligences

There are many ways besides IQ (intelligence quotient) to measure intellect. Dr. Howard Gardner, a psychologist, has identified seven kinds of intelligence which he calls multiple intelligences. Another psychologist, Dr. Thomas Armstrong says there are seven kinds of smarts. These different ways in which people are talented are listed below.

Circle all the ways you think you are smart or intelligent.

1. Musical Intelligence	Music smart
2. Bodily-Kinesthetic Intelligence	Body smart
3. Interpersonal Intelligence	People smart
4. Intrapersonal Intelligence	Self-smart
5. Visual-Spatial Intelligence	Picture smart
6. Linguistic Intelligence	Word smart
7. Logical-Mathematical Intelligence	Logic smart

True Colors

Dr. Daniel Goleman says we also have an EQ (emotional quotient)—your ability to handle your emotions. He believes it is the most important form of intelligence because it determines how happy and successful you will be.

Exercise 8

True Colors & Intelligence

Your true colors are another method of understanding how you are smart. Each color is intelligent in a different way. Your first color represents your major strengths and your unique kind of smartness. Below discuss your special talents and how that relates to your career choice. (Your TC cards can be helpful.)

Blue Intelligence

_____

_____

_____

Green Intelligence

_____

_____

_____

Gold Intelligence

_____

_____

_____

True Colors

Orange Intelligence

_____

_____

_____

Exercise 9

The Need to Manage Your Weaknesses

The most well rounded people have developed several parts of their personality—areas that need to be managed in order to be successful. Consider which of the areas above you need to strengthen so that you are more well rounded in things such as work, finances, and relationships. Since your last color represents your most challenging areas, use the space below to discuss what you need to do to improve in that area.

Example: My last color is gold. I need to work on balancing my checkbook and organizing my desk.

My last color is _____.

What I need to do to strengthen this area in my life is _____

_____

_____

_____

_____

True Colors

Chapter 10

Short Journal (5 minutes of less)

What new insights do you have about the way you learn best?

_____

_____

_____

_____

_____

_____

_____

_____

_____

_____

_____

_____

_____

_____

_____

_____

True Colors

> *The tragedy of life doesn't lie in reaching your goal. The tragedy lies in having no goal to reach.*
> — Benjamin E. Mays

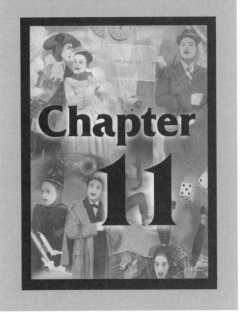

Chapter 11

DECISION-MAKING & GOAL-SETTING

Chapter 11

Decision-Making and Goal-Setting

Goals are the things that you want to accomplish because they have meaning to you. They should be realistic enough for you to believe they are possible, but at the same time not compromise your dreams. Some goals are short-term while others are long-term. A short-term goal might be to get a good grade in your higher math class so that you can accomplish a long-term goal of being accepted into a university.

Now that you have gained more knowledge about yourself and what you desire in your life, it is time to make it happen. Only you can take responsibility for your own life and accomplish your goals. It is important to keep a positive mental attitude that says "yes, I can." If you believe you can—you can! Of course, the opposite is also true. If you believe you can't—you are also right. It's your choice.

Exercise 1

Most desirable career

Take the most desirable choice from your list of 5 top careers in chapter 7, and complete the following exercise which includes some of your short-term goals.

Career Choice _____

This career is my first choice because _____

_____

_____

_____

_____

True Colors

What I need to do within 6 months to accomplish my goal is _____

_____

_____

_____

_____

_____

What I need to do within 1 year to accomplish my goal is _____

_____

_____

_____

_____

_____

The barriers I need to overcome to reach my goal are _____

_____

_____

_____

_____

_____

I plan to achieve my goal by _____(date).

True Colors

Exercise 2

Personal goals

While making decisions about the direction you want to take in your life don't forget to include personal goals. Balance in your personal and professional life is very important. You are not just a human being that has physical needs. You also have mental, emotional and spiritual needs. Make a list of your goals that address more of your personal needs.

Example: I will exercise 3 times a week, or I will listen to a motivational tape everyday for inspiration.

1. _____

2. _____

3. _____

4. _____

5. _____

6. _____

7. _____

Exercise 3

Long-term goals

It is also important to set long-term goals—those that take more time to accomplish. The more goals you can set for your life the more direction you will have.

Can you think of other goals you would like to accomplish in:

5 years

1. _____

2. _____

3. _____

4. _____

5. _____

10 years

1. _____

2. _____

3. _____

4. _____

5. _____

20 years

1. _____

2. _____

3. _____

4. _____

5. _____

True Colors

Exercise 4

My legacy

What Legacy do You Want to Leave?

One way to set goals is to look backwards. What contribution would you like to make that continues to benefit others long after your lifetime? Use the space below to write your legacy. It may generate more goals to add to your list.

_____

_____

_____

_____

_____

_____

_____

_____

_____

_____

_____

_____

True Colors

Hitch your
wagon to a star.
— Ralph Waldo Emerson

_____

_____

_____

_____

_____

_____

_____

_____

_____

_____

_____

The Need for Lifelong Learning

Old paradigms in the workplace don't apply anymore. The future trend is for workers to have several temporary jobs rather than one permanent one. This puts you in a position of always seeking new opportunities for which you need to have a competitive edge.

You must be responsible for your continuous learning and keeping your skills up-to-date. Companies are no longer sharing in this responsibility. They expect you to do whatever is necessary on your own time. Be prepared to take courses and workshops, read books and journals, and develop new skills.

True Colors

Exercise 5

Lifelong learning goals

The best time to prepare for lifelong learning is now. Think about and list below some other ideas for your continuous growth.

Example: additional degrees, start a foundation, write a book.

_____

_____

_____

_____

_____

_____

_____

_____

_____

_____

_____

_____

_____

True Colors

Recommendations

1. Read Carolyn Kalil's companion book **Follow Your True Colors to the Work You Love** for a better understanding of yourself and your ideal career.

2. Develop a resume. The purpose of your resume is to let potential employers know that you are interested in interviewing for an available job opportunity. Visit a career center to learn about necessary content and format options. Electronic resumes are becoming quite popular.

3. Learn interviewing techniques. See a career counselor to improve your interviewing skills.

4. Contact True Colors, Inc. for information about other products and training.

True Colors

Also available from True Colors:

Follow Your True Colors To The Work You Love
ISBN 1-893320-28-6

This text book is at the heart of the **Follow Your True Colors to the Work You Love** series. Carolyn Kalil, M.A., takes the mystery and misery out of your search for satisfying work, and helps you discover your natural strengths and talents with the help of the True Colors method. Learn to create a more positive self-image, overcome fears that block success, maximize your unique strengths, and more! 200 pages.

TCP-218-A. **$19.95***

Follow Your True Colors To The Work You Love: Instructor's Guide
ISBN 1-893320-22-7

The **Instructor's Guide**, written by career counselor Carol Imai, provides the necessary foundation to successfully guide students through **Follow Your True Colors To The Work You Love: The Workbook**. Filled with "required" exercises that are integral to the structure of the course, this dynamic resource also provides an array of optional activities that can be modified to accommodate your interests, needs, and the length of your course. 192 pages.

TCP-218-IG **$85.00***

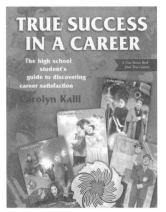

True Success in a Career
ISBN 1-893320-24-3

Written specifically for today's teens, **True Success in a Career** introduces high school students to the True Colors process and guides them toward careers that fit with who they are. Author Carolyn Kalil leads students through a journey of self-discovery to help them gain a better understanding of their natural strengths and identify careers in which they will find true satisfaction. 112 pages.

TCB-030. . . . . **$11.95***

* Plus shipping and handling